SWARTHMORE LECTURE 1963

# THE SWARTHMORE LECTURES

1940. THE LIGHT OF CHRIST IN A PAGAN WORLD
    *by John A. Hughes*

1941. THE UNDIVIDED MIND
    *by E. B. Castle*

1942. THE LAW OF LIBERTY
    *by Margaret M. Harvey*

1943. PLANNING FOR FREEDOM
    *by Leyton Richards*

1944. MAN, SOCIETY AND RELIGION: AN ESSAY
    IN BRIDGE-BUILDING
    *by W. Russell Brain*

1945. WORSHIP AND SOCIAL PROGRESS
    *by Wilfred Allott*

1946. THE WARRANT FOR YOUTH'S SEARCH
    *by John Hoare*

1947. THE SALT AND THE LEAVEN
    *by John W. Harvey*

1949. AUTHORITY, LEADERSHIP AND CONCERN
    *by Roger C. Wilson*

1950. JUSTICE AND THE LAW OF LOVE
    *by Konrad Braun*

1951. QUAKERISM: A FAITH FOR ORDINARY MEN
    *by R. Duncan Fairn*

1952. PREPARATION FOR WORSHIP
    *by Thomas F. Green*

1953. REMOVING THE CAUSES OF WAR
    *by Kathleen Lonsdale*

1954. FROM LONELINESS TO FELLOWSHIP
    *by Wilhelm Aarek*

1955. WHERE WORDS COME FROM
    *by Douglas V. Steere*

1956. QUAKERS AND THE RELIGIOUS QUEST
    *by Edgar G. Dunstan*

1957. QUAKERISM AND EARLY CHRISTIANITY
    *by Henry J. Cadbury*

1958. THE CONCRETE AND THE UNIVERSAL
    *by Margaret B. Hobling*

1959. THE CASTLE AND THE FIELD
    *by Harold Loukes*

1960. THE CREATIVE IMAGINATION
    *by Kenneth C. Barnes*

1961. TOLERANCE AND THE INTOLERABLE
    *by Richard K. Ullmann*

1962. BUILDING THE INSTITUTIONS OF PEACE
    *by J. Duncan Wood*

SWARTHMORE LECTURE 1963

# GOD IN EVERY MAN

BY

L. HUGH DONCASTER

LONDON
GEORGE ALLEN & UNWIN LTD
MUSEUM STREET

FIRST PUBLISHED IN 1963

PRINTED IN GREAT BRITAIN
*in 11 on 12 point Baskerville type*
BY HEADLEY BROTHERS LTD
109 KINGSWAY LONDON WC2
AND ASHFORD KENT

# PREFACE

The Swarthmore Lectureship was established by the Woodbrooke Extension Committee at a meeting held December 7th, 1907; the minute of the Committee providing for "an annual lecture on some subject relating to the message and work of the Society of Friends". The name "Swarthmore" was chosen in memory of the home of Margaret Fox, which was always open to the earnest seeker after Truth, and from which loving words of sympathy and substantial material help were sent to fellow-workers.

The Lectureship has a twofold purpose; first, to interpret further to the members of the Society of Friends their Message and Mission; and, secondly, to bring before the public the spirit, the aims and the fundamental principles of Friends. The Lecturer alone is responsible for any opinions expressed.

The Lectures have usually been delivered on the evening preceding the assembly of London Yearly Meeting of the Society of Friends in each year. The present Lecture, in abridged form, was delivered at Friends House, Euston Road, on the evening of May 24th, 1963.

A list of previous Lectures, as published in book form since 1940, will be found at the beginning of this volume, and those prior to 1940 at the end.

# BIOGRAPHICAL NOTE

L. HUGH DONCASTER was born in a Quaker family. His formal education was at two Friends' schools, where his interest in natural history was fostered, and at Cambridge University, where he took a degree in Natural Science. After a year of part-time teaching and part-time organizing of workcamps in the "depressed areas" of the 1930's, he went to do educational and social work among unemployed men in the Rhondda Valley, where he was greatly influenced by William M. Noble and George M. Ll. Davies. Here, he considers, his real education was given, and here he fell in love with Wales, the Welsh people and (especially) the Welsh sheep dogs. With his wife he visited many Friends' Meetings when Travelling Secretary of the Young Friends Central Committee, and they spent a period as caretakers of the Friends Meeting House in Cardiff. For the last twenty years he has been associated with Woodbrooke, latterly dividing his time between it and a smallholding.

# CONTENTS

| | | | |
|---|---|---|---|
| | *Introduction* | *page* | xi |
| I | *What Is That of God in Every Man?* | | 1 |
| II | *The Quaker Attitude to Theological Statement and to Creeds* | | 22 |
| III | *Friends and Christian Unity* | | 40 |
| IV | *Friends and the World Religions* | | 48 |
| V | *Is Quakerism for the Many or the Few?* | | 57 |
| VI | *What Think We of Christ?* | | 69 |

# GOD IN EVERY MAN

Friends all, everywhere, in the life and power of God live and dwell and spread the truth abroad. Quench not the spirit, but live in love and unity one with another, that with the wisdom of God ye may all be ordered to God's glory. And live all in patience one with another, and in the truth, that ye may feel and see to the beginning, before the world and its foundation was, in the faith which gives the victory; that nothing may reign but the life and power amongst you. And live all as the family of God in love, in life, in truth, in power, having your house established atop of all the mountains and hills, that ye may answer *that of God in every man*, and the word of the Lord ye may witness to go forth among you and be among you.

So in this the Lord God almighty preserve you and keep you. And in the Son of God's power live, for all power in heaven and earth is given to him, who is to subdue all the powers of darkness, and to make the kingdoms of the world his kingdom.

And none go beyond the measure of the spirit of God, nor quench it; for where it is quenched, it cannot try things. So if any have anything upon them to speak, in the life of God stand up and speak it, if it be but two or three words, and sit down again; and keep in the life, that ye may answer *that of God in every man* upon the earth. To you this is the word of the Lord God.

(George Fox, Epistle No. 150, 1657. Italics mine.)

# INTRODUCTION

THE terms of reference of the Swarthmore Lecture are that it shall deal with some subject relating to the faith and practice of the Society of Friends. When I was invited to give this lecture, I was asked to avoid historical analysis and generalization, and, as far as possible, to make it a personal statement of faith. My aim is therefore to try to present in my own terms matters which I consider to be essential Quaker faith and practice, with more of the first person singular than I would have chosen, but in the belief that in spite of my singularity it could often be replaced by the first person plural.

I have chosen this theme, that of God in every man, because it raises several issues on which there is at present wide divergence and much discussion within the Society of Friends, but over which there is no need for us to be at loggerheads. My aim is to try to describe in my own untheological language and thought form what I conceive that of God in every man to be, and then to consider very briefly some of its implications in five controversial fields.

First, there is the tension between those who wish for more theological definiteness and precision in the thinking of Friends, and those who believe that a religion based on personal experience must be flexible and comprehensive even if it runs the risk of being woolly and containing contradictions.

Second, there is the problem of the relationship of Friends to the rest of the Christian church, and particularly to the World Council of Churches, some Friends wishing us to be members of that body and others being equally clear that at present we should remain outside.

Third, there is the relation of Friends to the non-Christian faiths, some emphasizing Quaker universalism and others Christian particularism.

Fourth, there is the recurring question, Is the Society of Friends a fellowship in which many may be expected to find their spiritual home, or is it necessarily only for the few?

Finally, there is the age-old question, What think ye of Christ? which sometimes precipitates controversy between trinitarian and unitarian Friends, and sometimes emerges in other forms.

To touch on so much in so short a time may be foolish and even dangerous. It is foolish to try to enter into such large questions so briefly, when each could rightly have a lecture devoted to it; and it is dangerous in that what I say may touch off once again all our major controversies at one moment. It is my belief, however, that these issues are live ones, constantly near the surface of our Quaker thinking, and that instead of leaving them uneasily unresolved, we should fearlessly look at them together. In my own naïve thinking, which likes to have the best of every world, I believe there is room for much diversity within the Society, and that issues which tend to be forced into an either-or controversy very often can be seen more truly in a both-and context.

Consequently, although I know that I am likely to be under strong criticism from either side, I intend this lecture as a small contribution towards unity in the Society.

I have chosen for my title one of many phrases used by Friends to describe their religious experience. This one has become a Quaker cliché, hackneyed by much unthinking use. But it is a good phrase and deserves refilling with rich content, especially as it is likely to remain current among us. It is particularly character- istic of Fox. Neave Brayshaw records that he has found the thought of answering that of God in every man some sixty times in Fox's writings,[1] and it is familiar to Friends particularly in his oft-quoted letter to minister- ing Friends written from Launceston gaol in 1656:

> And this is the word of the Lord God to you all, and a charge to you all in the presence of the living God, be patterns, be examples in all your countries, places, islands, nations, wherever you come; that your carriage and life may preach among all sorts of people, and to them. Then you will come to walk cheerfully over the world, answering that of God in everyone; whereby in them ye may be a blessing, and make the witness of God in them to bless you.[2]

But in recent years this phrase has been under criticism, sometimes very weighty criticism. It is all too easy to shelter behind its vagueness. H. G. Wood well reminded us in 1951 that "we are still too easily satisfied with vague talk about something of God in every man",[3] and he repeated the reminder in 1955:

> It helps us little to say we believe in that of God in every man, if we do not know what we mean by "that" and what we mean by "God". Is the God whom we worship the Unknown God of the Athenian altar, or is he the God and Father of the Lord Jesus?[4]

[1] A. Neave Brayshaw, *The Personality of George Fox*, 1933, p. 18.
[2] George Fox, *Journal*, ed. J. L. Nickalls, 1952, p. 263.
[3] H. G. Wood, *Theology and Prayer*, 1951, p. 5.
[4] H. G. Wood, *The Quaker Understanding of the Christian Faith*, 1955, p. 9.

As he rightly says in the same context, "Personally I believe the directive that John Wilhelm Rowntree gave us fifty years ago is the right one. He reminded us that "the doctrine of the Inward Light upon which the tongue trips so lightly, requires searching elucidation."

It is as a small contribution to that elucidation that I now ask myself the question, What is that of God in every man?

# I

# WHAT IS THAT OF GOD IN EVERY MAN?

ANY attempt to explain the essentials of Quakerism quickly involves the use of one or more phrases which are in common use among us. We speak, for instance, of the Light Within, the Inner Light, the Inward Light, the Light of Christ, Christ Within, the Seed, or that of God in every man. In each case we are using a phrase to denote something very real and enormously important, something which lies at the heart of our religious life and affects what we say and do and are. But just because we know that in some way it is connected with the Infinite, it is necessarily beyond definition; and it is no accident that all these and many other expressions are in use among us, because, with their slightly differing emphases, they indicate the variety of approach to one reality.

When definition is impossible, we can still describe notable characteristics. I cannot define George Fox, but I can tell something of his strengths and weaknesses, of what he did and how he makes his impact upon me. In a similar way I can try to describe some of the characteristics of that of God in every man as I understand them and as I believe they have been known to Friends throughout their history. This I propose to do under five headings.

a. *Experience*

Clearly this that we speak of in so many different

metaphors is something known in our actual experience. It is not an idea thought up by the busy thinking mind, but something known personally in the depths of our being, involving of course the mind, but also the feeling and the will. "This never came out of the brain-beaten stuff of man, nor of his chamber of imagery", wrote Fox, and this is not what, on another occasion, he termed "brain-beaten heady stuff".[1] On the contrary, "This I knew experimentally" is his great affirmation, and should likewise be ours.[2]

And what did he know? What do we know? What do I know? First let me make it clear that when I say that this is known in experience, I do not mean simply in an experience which can be dated, though it may include vital, memorable events which stand out as beacons. But I am thinking of continuing experience, and therefore of varying experience, experience which grows and deepens. It is the whole person's experience, and may be known primarily in felt emotion, in decisions of the will sustained in disciplined living, and in the intellectual discoveries of thought. All these, separately and mixed together, are involved in our experience of God.

Such personal experience will vary from person to person, and for one person from time to time. It may begin, as it did for me, with no more than the recognition that love and truth matter supremely. It was simply the recognition of and surrender to values, with no awareness of God as a being, and frank refusal to conceive of him as personal and purposive. But this was surely the working of that of God in me. It was a live growing point. Neave Brayshaw's frequent quoting of the opening

[1] George Fox, *Epistles*, Nos. 293, 275.
[2] George Fox, *Journal*, ed. J. L. Nickalls, 1952, p. 11.

2

sentence of one of Fox's earliest letters[1] was advice both acceptable and practical. "Mind that which is pure in you to guide you to God." And as "that which is pure" has been minded experience has grown, and though that early beginning has never been rejected, bit by bit my understanding and awareness of God has filled out the picture, so that I understand (though I could not use for myself) the words of H. G. Wood when he writes of the inward light as "an experience of a transforming friendship which will make us to be what we know we are not yet".[2]

This experience of God grows or dwindles according to our faithfulness in "minding that which is pure". This needs underlining, and I propose to do so in some beautiful words of James Nayler, written from prison and growing out of the terrible reality of his own experience.

> As thou becomest faithful thereto, thou wilt feel the fruit of that Holy One springing in thee, moving to be brought forth in thee towards God and man . . . which if thou willingly serve in its smallest motion, it will increase, but if thou quench it in its movings, and refuse to bring it forth, it will wither and dry in thee, not being exercised.
>
> And it is the like of gentleness, meekness, patience and all other virtues which are of a springing and spreading nature, where they are not quenched . . . and will daily increase with using; but if thou wilt not give up for his name sake, but would hold the treasure and escape the reproach, then will it be taken from thee . . .
>
> What a glory is it to see
> Peace shine in the midst of war,

[1] George Fox, *Epistles*, No. 4 (*c.* 1651).
[2] H. G. Wood, *What do we mean by the Inward Light?* F. Q. E., 1930, p. 211. Reprinted as a pamphlet, p. 15.

2A

> Love in the midst of hatred,
> Meekness in the midst of strife,
> Righteous judgement in the midst of wickedness,
> Innocency in the midst of violence and oppression;
> As a lily amongst thorns, so is that of God amongst the
> men of the world.[1]

My first point, then, is that that of God in every man is known personally and inwardly and presently by each one of us, and so far it may be very individualistic and subjective. What is it that gives this inward experience objectivity and saves the Society of Friends from the anarchy of individualism and Ranterism? A large part of the answer lies in my second heading, Christ.

### b. *Christ*

For Friends the character of the inward light has always been related to Jesus Christ. In speaking of this deep inward experience they have often referred to it as the Light of Christ, or, quite simply, as Christ within. The inner light has not been just the light of reason or conscience, and still less has it been a case of your light and my light. It is the Light of Christ. He makes its character and content plain. In him it shines supremely, so that his character is its character, and that which we see only faintly in one another and ourselves, we see shining clearly in him. He is the Light of the World.

At the end of this lecture we shall look more closely at the significance which attaches to the word "Christ". At this point I simply wish to emphasize that when we speak of God, we refer to the God who is revealed to us supremely by him and in him. As Neave Brayshaw wrote in 1915:

[1] James Nayler, *How Sin is strengthened and how it is overcome*, 1657, reprinted in his *Works*, 1716, p. 370, where it is all printed as prose.

4

By far the greater part of any "inner light" that we know is, ultimately, whether we recognize the fact or not due to Jesus of Nazareth and to the Scripture; and our spiritual life is hurt by a confused thinking that leads to any neglect of these, setting the Light over against them as if it were their rival and superior.[1]

This necessitates a brief digression to consider our attitude to the Bible. Though "immediate revelation" was a phrase beloved of our forbears, and one which contains an important emphasis, in fact most of our experience is mediated to us through the insights of others. The Bible is a rich treasury of such experience and insight, and is supremely important as the source of our knowledge of Jesus Christ. It is therefore unthinkable for Quakerism to be divorced from the Bible. In fact, because of the danger of individualism, Friends need biblical knowledge even more than do other Christians.

The mutual relationship of personal and biblical insight is admirably expressed by Kathleen Carrick Smith.[2]

To interpret Scripture by the leadings of the Spirit, and to test those leadings by Scripture, in theory might appear a vicious circle. In practice it is rather a spiral climbing towards an ever fuller understanding of Scripture, and an ever clearer recognition of the Spirit.

Thus emphasis on experience, and on Jesus Christ, necessitates for Friends emphasis on the Bible which is the source of our knowledge of him.

I conclude this section on the Light known as experience of Christ by quoting once more from H. G. Wood:

[1] A. N. Brayshaw, *Memoir and Selected Writings*, 1941, p. 67, quoted in *Christian Faith and Practice*, 1960, 175
[2] Kathleen Carrick Smith, *The Church and The Churches*, 1948, p. 17, acknowledging a debt to Geoffrey F. Nuttall for the simile.

5

If we still claim to be and still intend to be a Christian Society, then it is clear to me that we must have a firmer grasp on the ultimate connection between our faith in something of God in every man and our faith in the divine humanity of Jesus Christ. We cannot rightly hold either faith without the other. If we are to have a message for today, we shall need to be true to the two foci of faith and to realize that they are inseparable.[1]

## c. *Universal*

My next heading may appear to be contradictory to the last, but it is a fundamental part of Quaker testimony that God's light shines in the heart of *everyone*: young and old, man and woman, sinner and saint, capitalist and communist, Christian and non-Christian.

In an early passage in Fox's *Journal* this universal element is well expressed.

> Now the Lord God hath opened to me . . . that every man was enlightened by the divine light of Christ; and I saw it shine through all, and that they that believed in it came out of condemnation and came to the light of life and became the children of it, but they that hated it, and did not believe in it, were condemned by it, though they made a profession of Christ.[2]

In a letter addressed to Friends who were captive in Algiers many years later, he urges them to answer God's witness in the Turks, Jews and Moors, continuing,

> And Friends, it would be very well for you, if you could get the Turks' and Moors' language, that you might be the more enabled to direct them to the grace and spirit

[1] H. G. Wood, *Theology and Prayer*, 1951, p. 7.
[2] George Fox, *Journal*, ed. J. L. Nickalls, 1952, p. 33.

of God in them, which they have from God, in their hearts.[1]

A less familiar passage, rather earlier, puts this universal emphasis most clearly. He is writing to Friends in America, some of whom have African slaves, and some of whom are in close relation to the Indians.

> Do not slight them, to wit, the Ethyopians, the Blacks now, neither any man or woman upon the face of the earth, in that Christ died for all, both Turks, Barbarians, Tartarians and Ethyopians; he died for the Tawnes and for the Blacks, as well as for you that are called Whites . . . and therefore now you should preach Christ to your Ethyopians that are in your families, that so they may be free men indeed, and be tender of and to them, and walk in love that ye may answer that of God in their hearts . . . that so they may come to know Christ, the Saviour, from whence grace and light comes.[2]

This raises explicitly the possible contradiction between the emphasis on Christ and that on universality. How can the light of Christ be known to those who have never heard of him? I cannot do better than quote Neave Brayshaw at this point.

> The early Friends identified this principle—the Light, as they called it—with Jesus Christ. It was not for them an impersonal abstraction, a substitute for God or Christ; for them it was *Christ*, manifesting Himself in the hearts of men; it was He whom the heathen, obedient to the Light, were obeying, even though they had not heard of His earthly existence, a more eminent mani-

[1] George Fox, *Epistles*, No. 388
[2] George Fox, *Gospel Family Order*, 1676, p. 13.

7

festation of Himself than any other. This is the Logos
doctrine of the gospel of John.[1]

They found other biblical support for this conviction
in, for example, I Peter I. 11, in which the spirit of
Christ is explicitly referred to as being at work in the
prophets.

It will be noted, however, that Fox does not conclude
that there is no need to preach Christ to those who do
not know of his earthly existence. Far otherwise. The
emphasis on that of God in *every* man provides a powerful
missionary motive. In the last passage just quoted from
him he quite explicitly says, "Therefore now you should
preach Christ . . . ", and the certainty that the Christ
spirit is already at work in the hearts of all men makes
more likely a positive response to this preaching. As
Henry Hodgkin reminded us in his Swarthmore Lecture
nearly fifty years ago, "The missionary spirit that is
distinctive of Christianity is essentially universal . . .
There is nothing for any man unless there is something
for every man in the Gospel of the Love of God."[2]

This can be put in another way by using a phrase
which was often used by the early Friends—that the
Light was given *in measure* to every man. To all men the
Light is given in measure, but in Christ it shines fully so
that he is the Light of the World. Penn takes this thought
furthest when he writes of the Light as saving, but Jesus
as Saviour; the Light as redeeming, but Jesus as
Redeemer; the Light as suffering, having to be crucified
and resurrected, all of which is embodied in Jesus

[1] A. N. Brayshaw, *The Quakers: Their Story and Message*, 2nd edition,
1927, p. 35, based on *Memoir and Selected Writings*, 1941, p. 64.
[2] H. T. Hodgkin, *The Missionary Spirit and the Present Opportunity*, 1916,
p. 95.

Christ.[1] The Christ spirit has been slain from the foundation of the world, and throughout time has triumphed in resurrection.

Is that of God in every man the same as the Holy Spirit? Why is it that Friends use their own Quaker phraseology instead of using expressions familiar to the rest of the Christian church? From what I have already said it should be clear that there is a difference which is fundamentally important. The phrase "Holy Spirit" in orthodox Christian usage is primarily concerned with the activity of God in the world since the earthly life of Jesus, and is closely identified with him. (e.g. Acts 16. 6-7). The Quaker conception of that of God in every man is more universal, so that while most Christians would not speak of the Holy Spirit at work in Jeremiah, it is natural for Friends to speak of the Inner Light or even the Light of Christ in him.

In practice, for most of us living in the west, when we speak of the Light we are thinking of the Holy Spirit; but we keep the wider term to be able to include the activity of God in the human heart at all times and in all places, including those in which the historic Jesus is unknown or so presented as to be unacceptable.

Before leaving the universal character of the Light, it is right to notice that the affirmation that "that of God" is in fact "in every man" is not strictly deducible from our experience which cannot be of all men, but it is an affirmation of faith supported by our experience as far as that goes. Richard Ullmann writes,[2] "In its earliest formulations, the immediacy of experience had not yet hardened into something like a slogan: Jesus Christ

[1] William Penn, *The Christian Quaker*, 1674, pp. 99-103 (Chap. XX).
[2] R. K. Ullmann, *Friends and Truth*, 1955, pp. 31-32.

'speaking to *my* condition', 'that of God in *you*'—these are expressions of actual relationship; they bear witness to the real meeting between one man and God, one definite and perhaps continual encounter in time and place." He continues, suggesting that the phrase "that of God in *every man*" introduces doctrine: it is "a matter of belief, not of experience". (I would say, "a matter of faith, supported by experience".) He goes on, "As such it may be still a central part of our faith, of the truth we hold and to which we are committed. But it is truth not because we have experienced it exactly thus, but truth through our own existential decision, truth which the self chooses as true when in the encounter with Transcendence it has grown to full selfhood. In selfhood it becomes aware of the potential selfhood of its fellow-men and seeks authentic communication with them in 'answering that of God within them' ".

### d. *Sin*

There are two other characteristics of this inward experience which were shown to be fundamental in Rachel Hadley King's study of *George Fox and The Inward Light* (1940), which are also clear in the writings of most early Friends, and, I believe, in our own experience. Like the three we have already mentioned, they were discovered in experience—experience which in their case was deeply Christian—and not thought up as the implications of faith.

One of these is a heightened awareness of sin in our own life, coupled with an awareness of power from God to overcome sin. As we become aware of the Christ spirit at work in us, we stand under judgement. That which we have so far accepted or tolerated is seen to be wrong when judged by what we believe are his standards. At the same time, as the Christ spirit is allowed to grow, power flows into our lives from him.

Friends are often chided for a shallow optimism regarding human nature, which underrates the ghastly reality of man's capacity for sin. But Friends do not close their eyes to the evil in the world and think of men as angels. On the contrary, "the first operation of the Spirit towards man lying in . . . sin, is to convince him of the sin", as Penington puts it.[1] Light cannot be thought of apart from darkness, and Friends are as committed to the one as to the other. The Light shines in darkness. The one without the other has no meaning.

But it is not only the recognition of sin in ourselves and in others, individually and collectively, which comes as we are aware of the reality of God. "He that shows a man his sins is he that takes it away", as Fox told the trooper who visited him in Derby gaol.[2] As we turn in obedience to God, and let the Christ spirit be formed in us (Gal. 4. 19), we are reconciled to God. "Christ saves not as he stands without at the door knocking, but as he is let in", says Penington, and, elsewhere, "It is not the outward name but the inward life and power which is the Saviour."[3]

A beautiful statement of experience of this power of God that overcomes sin, is in the writings of James Naylor. I quote again from *How Sin is Strengthened and How it is Overcome*,[4] written from prison in 1657, the year

---

[1] Isaac Penington, *Works*, 1681, Pt. I, p. 50.
[2] George Fox, *Journal*, ed. J. L. Nickalls, 1952, p. 64.
[3] Isaac Penington, *Works*, 1681, Pt. I, p. 50; Pt. II, p. 335.
[4] Quoted from James Nayler's *Works*, 1716, p. 368, where it is printed as prose. My italics.

after his so-called "fall", minted in the crucible of his suffering.

> So thou that lovest holiness, it is near thee;
> Power over sin and Satan is near thee;
> Salvation is at hand.
> Go not forth to seek that abroad which thou hast lost in thy own house.
> He that reproves the wicked is with thee;
> He that is pure is thy peace:
> He that never consented to sin but stands a witness against it.
> If thou hast such a spirit in thee, thou hast the Spirit of Christ the Saviour. So take heed unto *him*, to believe in *him*, and to mind *his* leading, and to follow *him*; if thou part not from *him*, *he* will be thy everlasting peace and overruling power to subdue thy sins . . .

Without getting drawn further into a discussion of salvation, we may re-iterate that it is a characteristic of the inner experience we are describing to sensitize the conscience so that new standards become the only ones that matter, and to give access of power in proportion to our willingness to obey the leadings we receive.

e. *Unity*

The last characteristic which I wish to mention is unity. It is a fact of experience that faithful following of the Light leads us into unity with those who also seek to follow it. This may not be immediately achieved, and there are many issues on which sincere Christians all seeking God's will come to diametrically opposed conclusions; but it is nevertheless true that where there is humility and faithful obedience, difference is dissolved and unity is ultimately discovered. This is to be expected if we are all following the leadings of the same Light, but our differing backgrounds and prejudices make us slow to achieve unity on issues over which we begin widely separated.

This is in practice a very important part of our understanding of that of God in every man. If we take this seriously, as Friends do, we must be seeking for the will of God through other people's insights just as much as, and often very much more than, through our own. It should be a corrective to arrogance and an encouragement to patient humility to remember that God is revealing himself all the time to everybody, and not only to ourselves, and that through others' faithfulness we may know most clearly what his leading is. In this connection we may be helped by a remark of Prof. T. W. Manson which George Sutherland once reported to me, to the effect that the trouble with Friends is that they only accept the light if it comes through their own gasmeter! The remark had reference to Friends as a group within the Christian church, and in that context it deserves to be pondered, but we also all know the individual Friend of whom the same could be said. Such a one is really a Ranter rather than a Friend, since the Quaker understanding of the Light includes the affirmation that it leads into unity.

Belief that the Light leads to unity provides a further check against the dangers of subjectivism and individualism which we noted earlier. We then said that a large part of the answer lies in the Light being the Light of Christ. The remainder lies in the conviction that it leads into unity. In practice, when we believe that we are prompted by the Inward Light, we must be sure that the prompting is in accord with Christ's spirit and with the findings of a sincerely seeking group of his disciples.

Unity is not to be confused with uniformity. Unity in the Society seems to me rightly attainable only in a context of diversity. Uniformity of belief or action is numbing and tends to crush out life. There must be only limited corporate pressure towards such uniformity. But a company of people united in their loyalty to the Light of Christ in all will, through the encounter of sincerely held differing convictions, be kept in a healthy state of dependence on the Light rather than on a particular apprehension of its leading. On any one issue at any one time, there may be a central position with extremes at either side; and this diversity is needed within the group if this is to remain livingly responsive to the leadings of the Light. It is our experience that such uneasy, dynamic tension can fruitfully exist within a unity of common allegiance.

But having made this plea for unity in a context of diversity, it is necessary to add that the emphasis lies on unity. The Society of Friends exists to bear corporate testimony to a certain understanding of Christian faith and practice, and such corporate testimony requires individual faithfulness. Neave Brayshaw wrote of this plainly in 1915 when the Society had to face diversity of response to a war situation. After saying,

> It is of importance to note that even in that early day (1660) Fox conceived of the Society as having principles which those who professed to belong to it ought not to break. He regarded such profession of adherence as bringing with it certain obligations,

he quotes H. G. Wood,

> It is all-important for the understanding of Fox to remember that *he did not stand merely or chiefly for the*

14

*general principle of the Inner Light: he bore witness to the Inner Light as expressed in clear moral judgments and in a developing moral experience* . . . The Society of Friends, according to Fox, is not composed of all who claim to be led of God, nor yet of all who are so led, but of those who recognize certain definite leadings of the Inner Light and are prepared to be faithful to such leadings.

Neave Brayshaw later says,

We Friends are something more than a social or semi-religious club, all of us led in different directions. We exist not for ourselves but to make our contribution to the world in bearing witness to our belief, shown in our practice, that the Inner Light, followed with understanding, leads us to certain definite testimonies.[1]

I re-iterate: it is a fact of experience that faithful following of the Light leads us into unity with those who also seek to follow it.

———

The physicist, for purposes of description, may divide so-called white light into the various wave-lengths known to us as the different colours in the visible spectrum. But in our experience of white light we are not normally conscious of the different colours into which it can be broken. Similarly my division of the inward light into a spectrum of five different characteristics may have had its uses in helping us to see more clearly some of the features of this central experience, but it is important to return from analysis and put together the features we have looked at separately, if we are to answer the question, What do I mean by that of God in every man?

If I try to do this personally, and to answer in very

[1] A. N. Brayshaw, *Memoir and Selected Writings*, 1941, pp. 70, 72-73, 75. Cf. pp. 78-81.

simple terms, I find myself saying something like this. It is experience of God, whose character is revealed to us supremely and uniquely in Jesus Christ, experience which is knowable in measure by everyone always. There follows at once the corollary that it involves deep reverence for human personality, and commitment in all relationships to seek "to answer that of God in every man". It is thus seen not as a theological statement of belief, but as a practical working hypothesis of faith affecting our every relationship. If I really believe that in every person I meet there is "that of God", what a difference it makes! If I know that our meeting may help or hinder the growth of that inner life—that which integrates personality—what an opportunity and responsibility is there. It helps me to try to keep such meetings personal and not merely functional, to be patient when I might be exasperated, to listen more than to talk, to have faith in the potentialities that may not be immediately visible—for if there is an angel in disguise in every one, the disguise is sometimes exceedingly good.

Let me illustrate in a simple anecdote concerning my beloved friend George M. Ll. Davies from whom I learned most of what I know about answering that of God in others. When he was visiting Birmingham to speak at a meeting, he spent an hour with me in Woodbrooke before we went into town. As we travelled together in the bus, the conductress came for our fares, and I, in eager conversation, held up the money saying, "Two all the way, please", and continued unaware of her. Not so George. He looked up at her and said quietly, "You look tired. It must be a weary business standing on your feet all these hours." She brightened visibly; she was a person, whereas I had reduced her to a slot machine.

Or, since I have been asked to be personal, let me illustrate the practical outworking of this faith in that of God in every man in another anecdote. In the sad and dreary days of mass unemployment in the 1930's, I was working among unemployed men's clubs in the Rhondda Valley. One day I went into a club and was greeted by a harassed looking committee member: "O Hugh bach, thank God you've come. We've been telephoning all over the place to find you. Come in here now just." I was hustled into a small room where I found the whole committee sitting round a table with long faces. I tried to liven them up: "Well, what on earth has happened! You look as though you are planning an execution!" To which the chairman replied lugubriously, "That's just about it."

Then the story came out. Sam, the treasurer, had had an accident underground a few years before in which he had lost an eye, and been somewhat lamed for life. He had received compensation and unwisely received it as a lump sum. He was a bachelor and he took to drink. Whenever I met him at any hour he smelt of beer. The habit took hold of him and he drank his compensation money. The "dole" allowed no margin for drink, but the habit was insatiable. As treasurer, he had the weekly contributions of club members accumulating till the quarterly bills were due, and temptation was too great. Sam had used the money and the club was bankrupt.

I asked what they proposed to do, and they replied, "Prosecute." I asked what good that would do to them or Sam. They admitted that they would not get the money back, but at least it would show the rebels in the club that they did not condone Sam's action. The committee were mostly above middle age, and there was a strong minority of young men who might use this as a handle to unseat them, and then, of course, the club would go to ruin. The chairman became eloquent about their duty to the members not to give the least chance of criticism to the rebels. They must be downright and firm and go all the way to prosecution. Despondently I turned from club politics and the vested interests of power and tried another line. Several of them had been in prison; I challenged them, "Was it easier or more difficult when you came back? Would it help Sam or hinder him to prosecute?" They admitted it would hinder—but they had their responsibility. We discussed for an hour and then I left them for a while, saying, "It's your club, and you must decide. I believe that all of you want to be generous. I'll be back in a couple of hours and you can tell me what you've decided."

When I returned the deadlock remained, but it was solved by a suggestion which pleased everyone but me. A general meeting of the whole club was to be called for the next night, at which the chairman would tell the members what had happened, would tell them that the committee was clear that Sam must be prosecuted, but would also tell them that I wanted to say something to them—so that if, by some happy chance, Sam was to be treated generously, the committee could not be blamed for weakness but could have the credit for allowing that possibility.

The next night I entered the billiards room with the chairman in an unnatural and frightening stillness in which the proverbial pin would have clattered if it had dropped. All down one side sat the committee; opposite them sat the rebels. 250 men were packed into the room, many standing, and hardly one could raise a smile of greeting. Again I thought of the courtroom and a sentence of execution. The chairman was commendably brief, and then threw me to the lions.

All I could do was to tell them a story. At a workcamp in Lancashire organized by Jack Hoyland I had visited an unemployed men's hostel in which 17 men shared a small house and by sharing its expenses made their meagre dole stretch a little further. One night a man broke in and was taking money from the till when caught by a policeman. He was taken to court and the chairman of the hostel was asked to be present to give evidence. The man had never had a chance in life: his parents were constantly drunk, and as a small child he had been turned on the streets to beg or steal his food. He had constantly been in trouble for petty theft. The case stood thus when the chairman was called to give evidence. He said that he had been asked to say on behalf of all his members that they were prepared to take the man into the hostel, to try to find him better clothes, and that the first one to find a job would, if it were possible, try to get it given to this man. The magistrates gave him a nominal sentence which had already been served, and he walked out free with the chairman.

There was still intense silence, but no longer so hostile. I continued my story. He lived with them, was found a job, and went straight for a longer period than ever before—but then he lapsed again into petty dishonesty. "That was what they did in Lancashire, and it didn't work—but it was right. What are you going to do?"

Once again I was conscious of the stillness in that

great crowd of normally so animated Welshmen, a stillness from which all trace of hostility had vanished. Presently a good old man broke the silence, "Well boys bach, there's only one thing for us to do," and a chorus of "Aye, aye" went up from all round the room including committee and rebels alike.

And so the great business of our lives becomes seeking to answer that of God in every man.

If we turn back from this practical and personal aspect, and consider the corporate implications in the life of the Society of Friends of our faith in that of God in every man, we shall notice that everything that is distinctly Quaker expresses this central conviction. Our unprogrammed worship allows full freedom to everyone present to be the channel through whom God's grace may flow to the other members of the group. Our meetings for church affairs are gatherings of the whole membership for the same reason. In both cases, and in other ways, women and men have fully equal opportunity. When we turn to our peace testimony, our social testimonies, our concerns for race relations and humanitarian service with its emphasis on "with" rather than "for", the same root is there. In daily living, the attempt to maintain one standard, a Christian standard, in *all* living on Sundays and Mondays, at home and abroad, in work and in leisure, in personal and social and political contexts, surely stems from and is nourished by the conviction that God is at work in the heart of every man, always, and it is our business to strengthen that life in him, everywhere, always.

In saying this, let it not be supposed that Friends thought up their doctrine of the inward light, and worked out its corollaries in logical sequence, and then concluded that "Quakerism" should consist of the resultant pattern. Far otherwise.[1] The pattern grew, and grows, according to the circumstances of the generation concerned, and new occasions evoke new responses. But those responses, insofar as they are true to the fundamentals of Quakerism, are developments in experience of faith in that of God in every man.

Having tried sketchily to indicate what I mean, and what I believe Friends mean, by that of God in every man, I now want to examine further three of the five characteristics I have mentioned, namely the universal element with special reference to its relation to experience and to Christ.

---

[1] Cf. H. J. Cadbury, *Answering that of God.* J. F. H. S., 39, 1947, pp. 3-14.

## II

# THE QUAKER ATTITUDE TO THEOLOGICAL STATEMENT AND TO CREEDS

a. *Theological Statement*

Emphasis on these three facets—*every man's experience of Christ*—leads at once to a characteristic attitude to precise theological definition. William Charles Braithwaite, whose scholarly writing so often expresses beautifully the fundamentals of our faith, says this of the early Friends.

> Religion for the first Friends was supremely an intercourse with the Divine, which set them in a place of vision and power and joy, and enabled them to see the things of time in the light of eternity. It was an experience which transformed the whole nature and gave new values to every part of life . . . The Friend had a life within him to wait on and to obey, not chiefly a creed to believe; and it was this life which developed in the Quaker groups a common body of truths to which they sought to bear unflinching witness. Accordingly they accumulated "testimonies" rather than Articles of Faith; and these were put into writing by way of advice to the church itself, and as a witness to the world; but were not at first thought of apart from the living experience behind them, which was the source of their authority. They represented a particular application of Truth expressed in life, not necessarily the final or perfect Truth.[1]

[1] W. C. Braithwaite, *The Second Period of Quakerism*, 1919, pp. 376-377.

They "accumulated 'testimonies' rather than Articles of Faith", or, as William Penn puts it tersely, they "placed religion in a clean conscience, not in a full head; in walking with God, more than in talking of Him".[1]

The history of our Book of Discipline illustrates this, and shows the characteristic attitude of the Society, changing in different circumstances. Until 1738 there was no volume to which reference could be made for the united judgements of the Society in matters of faith or practice. In that year, for convenience, manuscript volumes were prepared for the use of clerks of Quarterly Meetings. These contained, as their titles beautifully put it, "Christian and Brotherly Advices" concerned with how to live the Christian life, being extracts from Yearly Meeting minutes and epistles grouped under headings arranged alphabetically. They were practical counsels, and contained no statements of thought-out faith. This pattern was retained in the first three printed editions, though that of 1834, at the time of fiercest theological controversy in the history of Friends, introduced some statements of faith as an appendix to the Preface. This modest beginning paved the way for the great change which occurred in 1861, when the book was re-cast in the form of three chapters, the first being called Christian Doctrine. This consisted of fourteen extracts in chronological order and without sub-headings, four of them from the seventeenth and eighteenth centuries, and ten from mid-nineteenth century, designed to express the Quaker evangelical Christianity of that time.

[1] W. Penn, *The Christian Quaker*, 1674, Preface, Cf. George Fox, "the saints . . . were to walk as (the Son of God) walked and not only to talk as he talked: for there are too many talkers and few walkers in Christ; my desire is there may be more." *Epistles*, No. 353.

The changes in religious thought in the next sixty years were enormous. *The Origin of Species* was published in 1859, and our Book of Discipline in 1861 shows no evidence of this, which is natural enough. But while the practical parts of the volume (Christian Practice and Church Government) could be, and were, revised several times during the next two generations, it was not possible to revise this chapter on doctrine until the 1920's without risking a split in the Society. Even then the situation was extremely delicate, and without the sensitive wisdom of William Charles Braithwaite, there might still have been a serious crisis when the new volume came to be presented to Yearly Meeting, as differences on matters of doctrine were profound. How could one book satisfy both the orthodox evangelical and the liberal?

The answer was found in a return to characteristic Quakerism. Instead of presenting belief primarily in the form of theological statements, it was presented primarily in personal accounts of religious experience. Insofar as statements of belief of a theological character were deemed necessary, these were selected to be as representative of Quaker belief as possible in the age in which they were written, and each chapter contained a number of statements coming from various periods of our history. No attempt was made to iron out differences or even contradictions. The whole was presented as an anthology of Quaker thought and practice, prefaced by the noble postscript to the message issued from the first general meeting of Friends of a widely representative character, the meeting of elders at Balby in 1656:

> Dearly beloved Friends, these things we do not lay upon you as a rule or form to walk by, but that all, with the

24

measure of light which is pure and holy, may be guided;
and so in the light walking and abiding, these may be
fulfilled in the Spirit, not in the letter, for the letter
killeth, but the Spirit giveth life.

It will be seen that, apart from a period of sixty years
from 1861, there has been no time when any particular
formulation of faith has been held before the Society
authoritatively in our Book of Discipline. It will be seen
further that during that time the statements to which
Friends were committed were statements of a pro-
nouncedly evangelical character which were no longer
acceptable to most twentieth-century Friends, and the
new volume of *Christian Life, Faith and Thought* seemed
to the generation of 1920 to be a release from bondage
to outworn ideas.[1]

But this sets the stage for the tension that now exists
among us in relation to theological statement. Looking
back, there is no doubt that Friends were gravely wrong
in insisting on a particular theological orthodoxy in the
nineteenth century, and even in disowning those who
could not accept it. But in rightly reacting from this, there
has been a tendency to go so far in the opposite direction
that membership in the Society is sometimes thought to
involve no theological commitment, and there are even
a few reluctant to see the Society labelled as Christian.
Now, naturally, there is a reaction back again, many
Friends being dissatisfied with what seems to them to be
a vague, woolly liberalism without commitment to
anything more than "seeking", and such Friends eagerly
welcome more precise teaching about the facts of

[1] A somewhat extended account of these developments is contained in
an article of mine entitled, "Towards Revision of the Book of Discipline"
in *The Friends' Quarterly*, 1954, pp. 91f.

Christian faith, and would like the Society to state more explicitly where it stands.

There are, of course, dangers in both positions. H. G. Wood used to remind us that

> because Fox saw so clearly the inadequacy of beliefs held only by the top of the mind and not received into the heart, because he exposed the weakness of a religion of mere notions, we have sometimes been tempted to imagine that there is some virtue in having no notion of what we believe.[1]

If our personal faith remains unthought out and vague, it lacks dynamic power in our own lives, and we are prevented from communicating it to others; and this is true of our corporate, as well as of our personal, life.

On the other side there is the perennial danger of isolating belief—by which I mean the articulated, thought-out part of faith—from the whole of faith which involves the whole of personality. It is so fatally easy for us to think in terms of ideas and interpretations of facts as though they were the most important part of faith. Rufus Jones, after describing Quakerism as "a kind of Christianity which begins with experience rather than with dogma", comments on the change from the early position of Luther whose "saving faith is an inward attitude based upon first-hand experience" to the later Reformation in which "the acceptance and maintenance of sound doctrines became the essential condition of salvation. Faith . . . became synonymous with belief".[2] The same transition is abundantly clear if one compares the vital, heart-warming, personal experience of the

[1] H. G. Wood, *Theology and Prayer*, 1951, p. 5. Cf. *The Quaker Understanding of the Christian Faith*, 1955, p. 4.

[2] Rufus M. Jones, *The Faith and Practice of the Quakers*, 1927, 6th edition 1944, p. 44.

eighteenth- and early nineteenth-century evangelicals with the tendency of the later nineteenth century to emphasize correctness of doctrine. Faith, as Edward Grubb pointed out, can easily be reduced to "The Faith", a deposit of sound teaching.

> If faith is the response of our whole being to Christianity as Life, and Belief is the response of our intellect to Christianity as Truth, a similar difference will hold between the expressions of Christianity in religion and in theology."

And in this context he affirms, "Christians do not need uniting in matters of faith, for in these they are already one. Where they differ is in belief, which is a very different thing."[1]

This stress on faith as the response of the whole being is, of course, another way of putting the emphasis I have already made on experience. And this point of view is one which is intrinsically bound up with Quakerism. Early Friends often made distinctions between what they called head and heart knowledge, between the history and the mystery, between profession and possession. "We do distinguish betwixt the certain knowledge of God, and the uncertain; betwixt the spiritual knowledge, and the soaring, airy head-knowledge."[2] In this I am sure that Friends do not, in the end, differ from other Christians; but there is a different starting point and a different emphasis. "You will say Christ saith this, and the apostles say this, but what canst thou say?"[3]

---

[1] Edward Grubb, *Christianity as Truth*, 1928, pp. 19, 30, 24-25.

[2] Robert Barclay, *Apology*, 1678, II. l.

[3] George Fox, *Journal*, Bicentenary edition, 1891 and 1901, Vol. II. p. 512.

Edward Grubb puts this so well that I cannot do better than quote him at some length on this point. Writing of the early Friends, he says,

> Christianity was for them essentially an experience of the Light of Christ in the soul, and a way of life based on that experience. This was the primary thing, and correctness of belief, though not unimportant, fell into second place. They certainly did not mean that there was no common standard of true belief, any more than they meant that there was no common standard of right action. What I think they did mean . . . is that it is vain to attempt to safeguard the stronghold of Christian faith by a wire entanglement of human creeds. They were prepared to trust to Christian experience as the real safeguard against error. They believed that those who were really following the Light of Christ would (by a kind of instinct) accept ideas that nourished his life in the soul, and reject those that did not; and that so, if all the emphasis were laid on loyalty to Christ, correctness of belief would largely take care of itself.[1]

Does this mean that theology is unimportant? Clearly not. If theology is clear thinking about religious experience, then it is extremely important. If it is primarily clear thinking about religious experience as expressed in the Bible, it is still extremely important. The more clearly we can think, the more we can understand, the more we see the implications in practical living, and the more we are able to communicate to others. But while we must remember that thinking is a part of experience, we must not overlook feeling and willing, and religious experience is commitment of the whole man to God. The danger lies not in too much

[1] Edward Grubb, *What is Quakerism?*, 1919, p. 45; 6th printing, p. 42.

theology, but in claiming too much authority for the findings of the theologians.

There are two further comments which seem to me relevant here. The first is that theology, like clothes, has fashions. Fortunately its fashions do not change annually according to the whims of a fashion house in Paris, but at longer periods it naturally happens that those who are seeking to interpret in thought form and language that which is beyond final expression in words, must restore emphases which seem to have been lost. Consider, for example, the different ways in which "atonement" has been understood by Christians in different periods, the faith of one generation being shocking, even blasphemous, to the next. But the fact of Jesus at Calvary remains central, full of mystery and immense significance, so full that it can never be contained in a formula. Surely we must never make our interpretations sacrosanct. Physicists have explained light by the corpuscular and wave theories, and no doubt by many others, each of which had its uses; but light remains when the theories have become history.

The other comment is that if theology is clear thinking about religious experience, its value is in proportion as its findings are near to experience. Logical deductions may be made, but at two or three removes they may have come to be far removed from reality since they are concerned only with rational thought and omit much else in experience. The doctrines of election and reprobation as crudely taught in seventeenth-century England (and as still to be encountered in certain groups) could be arrived at by perfectly logical reasoning from the religious certainty of the sovereignty of God, but in their final form they seem more devilish than divine both in the character implied for God and the companionship foretold for unsaved man. Thus theology must be the handmaid of experience, but never its mistress. At the same time we must recognize that the doctrines of the church are attempts to express that which has been vital in the experience of the church, and any doctrine which we cannot at the moment accept must not be rejected out of hand, but seen as a challenge to deeper thinking as a part of deeper experience.

Some of the difficulties I have mentioned are illustrated in the unhappiest chapter of our Quaker history: the great split in America which is usually called the Hicksite controversy. There were a number of important factors underlying this, including the tensions between richer, more sophisticated, urban Friends, and poorer, simpler, rural ones: and between the office-bearers concerned for the Society's orthodoxy and discipline, and those who were seeking for more personal and individual freedom. But the actual encounter in the field of ideas which could be debated in speech and writing, resolved itself into controversy over three issues, which may be expressed in terms of three pairs. There was, first, the authority of the inward light versus the authority of the Bible. The Hicksites claimed that the inward light gave a complete, unerring, saving revelation of God, while the orthodox claimed that the Bible was the complete, unerring, saving revelation of God. This was closely tied up with the second pair, Christ within versus the Jesus of history. The Hicksites claimed that Christ saves within and in no other way, while the orthodox constantly stressed as, quite literally, crucial, the propitiatory sacrifice of Christ on Calvary. Beneath these two controversies lay a third, not quite so explicit: the emphasis on experience versus the emphasis on correct doctrine.

It is only necessary to formulate the issues in controversy in this way, to see how each side had been driven to testify to a great and fundamental truth, but, each in the stress of controversy, had been pushed so far in its defence that it had lost the firm grip necessary on the complementary position. Quakers at that time saw these pairs as antithetical, and synthesis was therefore impossible; whereas whenever Quakerism has been healthy, it has been realized that these exaggerated positions derive from complementary sides of one experience, which can no more be divided from each other without mutilation than can the opposite sides of a coin.

In practice, many of our controversial themes are of this kind. Truth is too great to be defined completely, and any attempt to formulate one aspect at once seems inadequate to those for whom another has been vitally important. I believe that our discussions of such subjects as the universalist and particularist trends in Quakerism, and the divinity and humanity of Jesus, are most truly to be seen as complementary to one another rather than as sharply defined alternatives. Each needs the other to prevent extremist unbalance.

Where does all this lead? If truth is of this kind, there will not be an exact centre which is "correct" while everything off-centre is "false". Rather we may think of it as a many-sided crystal which can only be seen in its wholeness by approach from every side. Each of us must approach truth in our own way from where we are. "The heart of so great a mystery cannot ever be reached by following one road only."[1] Richard Ullmann in his Swarthmore Lecture two years ago, rightly pointed out the inadequacy and even falsity of this physical analogy.

> Truth, the truth of which we are certain without ever knowing it, is not static like a statue, but is the bottomless truth of eternity that engulfs us and towards which we yearn. Even supposing we could add up all our glimpses of truth, it would still be no more than the sum of very human truths and not that one eternal truth.[2]

But we have to use pictures to convey meaning, even when we know they are inadequate.

With this caution in mind, let us think of the visible spectrum of light, showing the range of colours from red to violet, but continuing at either end in invisible infrared and ultra-violet rays. In such a figure, the Society of Friends may be represented by the visible colours, each representing a reality. There is a wavelength somewhere near the green (how fortunate?) which may be typical of the corporate pronouncements of the Society, but its members may have wavelengths shorter or longer, and beyond its borders are the invisible others still more extremely removed from each other. But, one should add, as generations come and go, the corporate position of the Society will move alternately towards the red or the violet. May we never become static even in the safety of the central green!

When H. G. Wood had described the vagueness, theological ignorance and uncertainty of some modern Quakerism, he continued, "This situation, if correctly diagnosed, does not call for the imposition of a creed,

[1] Symmachus, quoted by Kenneth Walker, *So Great a Mystery*, 1958, p. 11.
[2] R. K. Ullmann, *Tolerance and the Intolerable*, 1961, p. 52.

but it does summon us to mental fight."[1] If the present call for more precise theological teaching means a much greater mental effort to understand the religious experience of men and women as revealed to us in the Bible, in history, in one another and in ourselves, it is wholly to be welcomed. If in our attempt to understand such religious experience, we are led closely to examine the interpretations which have been given to it, our own experience is likely to be clarified and deepened. But if in this exercise of mind and spirit we are led to dogmatize and claim as sacrosanct any particular interpretation, even with biblical authority behind it, let us beware and be humble, remembering that our apprehension of truth is partial, and that many paths lead to God. "The heart of so great a mystery cannot ever be reached by following one road only."

William Charles Braithwaite has some very relevant counsel on this matter.

> Doctrinal belief, laying the emphasis in religion on an intellectual assent to Truth, was rightly regarded by early Friends as a barren substitute for a living, inward experience of Christ. As William Penn puts it, "It is not opinion, or speculation, or notions of what is true, or the subscription of articles or propositions, though never so soundly worded, that . . . makes a man a true believer or a true Christian; but it is a conformity of mind and practice to the will of God, in all holiness of conversation, according to the dictates of this principle of divine light and life in the soul, which denotes a person truly a child of God."
>
> . . . Clear thinking, however, has its important, though subordinate, part to play; for religion, as we are now learning, is a growth out of the whole nature of man, in

[1] H. G. Wood, *The Quaker Understanding of the Christian Faith*, 1955, p. 6.

which intellect, emotions and will are all concerned. Theological and philosophical statements are accordingly of high value, if so made as to satisfy such conditions as the following. Are they put forward not dogmatically but educationally, so as to bring the soul to its own great moments of discovery? Are they given as final verdicts, or only as provisional statements capable of further expansion? What inspiring experience of the church lies behind the necessarily imperfect words that are used? Above all, has the definition pressed out the life and wonder of the truth, or does it allow these to be felt?[1]

## b. *Creeds*

What I have been trying to say leads naturally to a consideration of our attitude to creeds, by which I mean brief, formal summaries of Christian doctrine, and such consideration may sum up this section.

We have already noted that until the nineteenth century there was no authoritative statement of faith held before Friends as enshrining "the belief" of the Society. Particular statements were made on particular occasions, by individuals and groups, and would undoubtedly have the assent of Friends generally. Only when Friends swung over to a markedly evangelical position in which correctness of doctrine was of paramount importance, did they bring such statements into prominence. It appears that it is only since the unhappy lessons of those days have been learned, that Friends have been corporately explicit concerning their attitude to creeds. This was formerly taken for granted, whereas now it is one of the formulated testimonies of the Society. But

[1] William Charles Braithwaite, *The Second Period of Quakerism*, 1919, pp. 379-380. The quotation from Penn is from *A Key*, etc., section 2.

this is no change of attitude, only an explicit statement of it, which repeats what may be found clearly stated in the first and second generations.

We have just quoted from William Penn. Thomas Story says the same, "The unity of Christians never did nor ever will or can stand in uniformity of thought and opinion, but in Christian love only."[1]

Nor did this attitude die with the early Friends. At the beginning of the nineteenth century, the Evangelicals among us were pressing for the publication of a Catechism in the name of the Society, and Meeting for Sufferings in 1809 refused to issue this because it entered too minutely into questions of doctrine.[2] A few years later there was a foretaste of the unhappy scenes which were to occur at the time of the great separation in American Quakerism, when there was an unsuccessful attempt by the Evangelicals to fasten what the Liberals considered to be a creed on to Philadelphia Yearly Meeting.[3] A third example of the same feature of Quaker experience even in the prevalent evangelicalism of the nineteenth century, is to be found in the significant refusals of Dublin and London Yearly Meetings to accept the Richmond Declaration of Faith in 1888.[4] And should anyone think that there is a great difference in principle between acceptance of a lengthy declaration of faith and acceptance of a creed, it remains true that the word "creed" occurs with considerable frequency in the record of the discussion in *The Friend*, and Thomas

[1] Quoted from *Christian Faith and Practice*, 1960, 221.
[2] *The Yorkshireman*, 1836, V. 97f.
[3] Bliss Forbush, *Elias Hicks*, 1956, pp. 218-221.
[4] This was a long evangelical statement of faith prepared and adopted at a conference of evangelical Friends representing European and some American Friends' Yearly Meetings, held at Richmond, Indiana, in 1887.

Hodgkin thought that Joseph Bevan Braithwaite would not be able to get very far if he were to try to distinguish between them.[1] The issue may have been different, but it was closely allied.

Thus it appears that, although the explicit testimony of the Society has been more obvious in recent years than earlier, it is but the expression of a conviction that is characteristic of Friends in each generation.[2] Why is it, then, that we do not ask our members to subscribe to any creed?

First, because emphasis on a creed puts first things second. This I have already tried to say at length. Faith is

> the response of a man's whole being to the love and grace of God when these are inwardly revealed to him. Faith is not only a belief in truth, but a surrender to truth ... To think that we have defined our faith when we have only defined the cognitive side of it, is to treat the definition of the less important part, as if it were the definition of the whole. If this partial definition be imposed as an "article of faith", the result can only be a Christianity of doctrines instead of a Christianity of experience.[3]

The worst disasters of Quaker history have come when "correct belief" has been given priority over faithfulness to "the promptings of love and truth in our hearts".[4]

Second, and this is saying the same in another way, a dynamic faith can never be adequately expressed in a static form of words. "While truth is eternal our

---

[1] *The Friend*, 1888, p. 160.
[2] For the history of Friends' attitude to creeds, see A. Mekeel, *Quakerism and a Creed*.
[3] *The Basis of Christian Unity*, 4th edition, 1940.
[4] *The General Advices*, I. 1.

apprehension of it enlarges, and our expression of it changes."[1] And though this is true and accepted by the upholders of creeds, the tendency of the human mind is to accept the statement as finally true. The French put it neatly, "Le Dieu défini est le Dieu fini." Whittier puts his finger unerringly on the point in two lines,

> From scheme and creed the light goes out ...
> The blessed Master none can doubt.[2]

Third, and again we are trying to say the same thing in yet another way, creeds tend to fetter the search for truth by crystallizing thought on matters beyond final embodiment in language, if, by insisting as they seem to do that this formulation is the one way towards truth, those who come by another route are excluded. It may well be that without the rediscovery of the humanity of Jesus by Biblical scholars, nineteenth-century Evangelicalism would have lost us the reality of the Incarnation, by so stressing the divinity of Christ that his humanity was no longer real. This is not as far fetched as it may sound. As I write these words I remember a student from an orthodox Christian home saying to me in Woodbrooke a few weeks ago, "Here I have for the first time discovered the humanity of Jesus, and it is wonderful!" Edward Grubb made the same point when he wrote, "The orthodox creeds, while nominally maintaining at once the divinity and humanity of Jesus, have in effect thrown the latter away."[3]

Thus it is that Friends, in their constant emphasis on the inwardness of religious experience involving the whole man, have never felt free to bind their members

[1] *Christian Faith and Practice*, 1960, 116.
[2] John Greenleaf Whittier, *The Friend's Burial*.
[3] Edward Grubb, *Authority and the Light Within*, 1908, p. 50.

to subscription to any credal statement which would emphasize belief more than the rest of faith, thought more than the rest of life. They have found through the centuries a very real corporate unity in a common experience of discipleship, a common knowledge of the life of God springing in the hearts of men, a common faith that obedience to the Light of Christ will lead into unity with one another and with him. If, to be considered a Christian, it is necessary to be able to affirm every clause of the Apostles' Creed, then there must be many Friends who do not qualify. If it means to want to be a follower of Jesus, then the Society of Friends is a wholly Christian body.

Such a position exposes us to very grave dangers. The refusal to set up an external standard of belief to which all must conform leaves room for untrue thinking, muddled thinking, and no thinking at all. Such a position itself may undercut the very commitment which we are seeking to maintain. It may prevent us from stating crisply and authoritatively just for what the Society stands. It may hinder us in our communication of our belief to others. It exposes us to such diversity within the body that contradictory positions may be found among us. To the outside observer, and to some among us, it appears confused and confusing, unclear and untidy. The great historic creeds of the Christian church have had immense value in safeguarding the church from drifting into dangers such as these.

But we believe that the response to such dangers is not the imposition of a creed but the summons to mental fight to which H. G. Wood has called us. To say that Friends have no creed is not to say that each Friend has no belief. Far otherwise. Each one, and each group, has the responsibility to seek, and seek, and seek again where the Light is leading; to find what the life of God means in the life of man; to wrestle with the great facts and mysteries in the heart of our Christian experience, and to know what we believe about them. It is only when we have formulated our faith for ourselves that we can communicate it to others or know its incisive power in our own day-to-day discipleship.

The position of Friends seems to me to be so closely parallel to that of Congregationalists as reflected in a quotation from *The Life of R. W. Dale of Birmingham,*[1] that I close this section with it. It comes from one of the preliminary notes to the Declaration of 1833 establishing the Congregational Union:

> Disallowing the utility of creeds and articles of religion as a bond of union, and protesting against subscription to any human formularies as a term of communion, Congregationalists are yet willing to declare, for general information, what is commonly believed among them, reserving to every one the most perfect liberty of conscience.

Friends also disallow the utility of creeds as a bond of union, and are yet willing to declare what is commonly believed among them, which we do in our *"Book of Discipline"* which is revised (apart from special circumstances which were noted earlier) approximately in every generation.

[1] A. W. W. Dale, *The Life of R. W. Dale of Birmingham,* 1898, pp. 343-4.

4B

# III

# FRIENDS AND CHRISTIAN UNITY

THIS consideration of the nature of the unity we know within the Society, leads naturally to looking at the same question in the wider context of Christian unity. It is not my purpose here to discuss the whole question of the relationship of Friends to the ecumenical movement in general, or to the World Council of Churches in particular; but the things I have just been saying about our own experience as Friends have a direct bearing on these matters.

The emphasis I have been making on *every man's experience* of *Christ*, to say nothing of the fact that this leads into unity, points quite clearly to a natural identification with our fellow Christians of other denominations, a realization of unity in a common Christian discipleship. It would be strange indeed if in our emphasis on that of God in every man, we failed to see its implications for us in relationships with fellow-Christians. It follows that in our search for deeper insights into the nature of that discipleship, we shall want to seek with them, to learn from their experience, to check the promptings of love and truth in our hearts with similar promptings in theirs. And this means real, close, personal relationship, corporately and individually. It is wholly right, therefore, that Friends should co-operate whenever and wherever they can in inter-church activity.[1]

[1] Perhaps we should note the striking difference between this attitude and that of Friends and other Christians in the seventeenth century. May

Such co-operation will reveal wide fields of common experience, some areas in which emphases are different, and some in which there is stark antithesis. These last will sometimes make it impossible for Friends to be identified with positions formulated by others, if they are to remain true to their own experience and the convictions arising from it. What we conceive to be the basis of Christian unity is sometimes one of these.

For Friends, and, I believe, for all Christians, the basis of Christian unity lies in a common experience of commitment to the inward leadings of the Christ spirit, God. It is in love of and loyalty to him that we are united.

> The unity of Christians is not something that needs to be created; it is already here, and needs only to be recognized and acted upon. All those who love our Lord Jesus Christ, and in whose lives his character is being manifested, know this inner unity, whatever diversities there may be in the formulas by which they express themselves, or in the practices by which they seek to cherish his life in their souls.[1]

This has been admirably expressed in a passage which stood in *Christian Practice* from 1925 till the revision of 1960:

> We find the true bond of Christian unity, not in any statement of our common faith, however carefully expressed, or however vital may be the doctrines set forth; not in any uniform system of church organization, not in any rite of which all partake. We find it rather in

[1] *The Basis of Christian Unity*, 4th edition, 1940.

it be that one of many factors underlying the change of outlook is the present greater emphasis on the experience of Christian discipleship rather than on the certainty of precisely formulated doctrinal and ecclesiastical positions believed to be finally true?

the participation in a common inner life springing out of communion between the human soul and God, and expressing itself in the daily life of those who experience it. We find ourselves in union with all who loyally follow our Lord and Saviour Jesus Christ, and who devote their lives to the extension of His Kingdom of righteousness and truth, in whatever way they may be led of the Spirit.[1]

To make acceptance of a statement of belief the *basis*, or the condition of membership, of any group of Christians is thus contrary to that which we have felt called to stress for three centuries.[2] To refuse to accept a credal basis, even when most Friends could for themselves subscribe to the words concerned, is not to strain at a gnat and swallow a camel, nor is it hair-splitting. We have a testimony here concerning the nature of Christian unity, and, indeed, of Christianity itself.

We have seen already why Friends do not require of their own members subscription to a creed. We may now affirm that in our judgement the use of a creed as the basis of Christian unity is wrong for three reasons:

First, it stresses one part, and not the most important part, of Christian discipleship. The unity of Christians depends not on their being able to express themselves in the same words, but on one divine life creating in men the life of God.

Second, a credal basis inevitably and intentionally acts like a fence which keeps people out, while a basis of Christian unity should be like a field inviting people in.

[1] Friends' Foreign Mission Association: Principles of Action, 1914. Quoted in *Christian Practice*, 1945, pp. 35-36.

[2] I recognize that unity between individual Christians and unity between Christian churches involve different considerations, but it appears to me that what is said here about the basis of Christian unity applies to both.

The more I have thought about it the more I have reluctantly come to the conclusion that the primary purpose of a credal basis is, in fact, that it should keep certain people out. This is borne out by the fact that the alternative which Friends suggest, "that it would be preferable to throw membership open to all Churches claiming to be Christian and expressing a desire to join in and to further the work of the Council",[1] is not acceptable apparently because it is too broad, too wide, too potentially inclusive. But "we affirm our conviction that diversity of experience and of emphasis should enrich and not weaken the common life".[2] As Henry Cadbury quoted in his Swarthmore Lecture,

> He drew a circle that shut me out—
> Heretic, rebel, a thing to flout.
> But Love and I had the wit to win:
> We drew a circle that took him in.[3]

Third, it seems to assume that there is but one gateway to Christian faith, and that until one has passed through it, one is not a Christian, while Friends believe that all who are "humble learners in the school of Christ"[4] are in measure united to him. The ultimate and only basis of Christian unity is in loyalty to him, and not in acceptance of a formula purporting to describe him.

When Friends of London Yearly Meeting reluctantly declined the invitation to join the World Council of Churches in 1940, they did so because they believed that

---

[1] *Proc. Y. M.*, 1940, p. 157.

[2] *The Basis of Christian Unity*, 4th edition, 1940.

[3] Quoted from Edwin Markham by H. J. Cadbury, *Quakerism and Early Christianity*, 1957, p. 33. This Swarthmore Lecture also pleads for freedom from theological uniformity, especially pp. 43-48.

[4] *Church Government*, 1931, chap. III, para. 16.

an important testimony was at stake. Their minute is worth recalling:

> It is our hope that our Society may find its place in fellowship, consultation, prayer and common work with our fellow Christians. While we are unable to accept the invitation which we have received, we do desire where possible to be in association with those who are seeking to draw together all Christians in deeper fellowship.[1]

It is my belief that this desire has to a large extent been realized in the years since it was expressed, both as between London Yearly Meeting and other bodies of Christians, and at the local and more personal level; and I believe this will continue increasingly to be the case. In such association we shall learn much that will humble us, and this is essential for our spiritual health since there is too much Quaker pride. But I trust that we shall never, for the sake of the possible advantages of organic unity, accept membership in any body whose "basis" singles out from Christian experience the element of belief as though it were paramount.

In this connection, an extract from an article by Canon Shepherd seems to me relevant.[2]

> When the early Church was faced by the question of possible Christian unity and fellowship with Gentiles, whose hearts Christ had won, but who knew nothing of the Jewish theological rites and dogmas that were the background of earlier Christian experience, the Council of Jerusalem (see Acts XV. 19) made no appeal to theology. That would inevitably have barred the way.

[1] *Proceedings of London Yearly Meeting*, 1940, p. 325.
[2] Article entitled "Getting Together" in *The Birmingham Post* of 16. xii. 1961, by Dr. A. P. Shepherd, Canon of Worcester.

Instead, they jettisoned as essential elements of Christian belief and practice rites and rules with a millennium of unquestionable theological authority—circumcision, temple-worship, observance of the Mosaic law, Sabbath observance and racial *Apartheid*—and appealed to one thing only, the immediate evidence as to how God was leading them in the new circumstances. This alone could bring the Christian Church into a world-wide fellowship. Theological logic would have split it into a Jewish sect and a gnostic heresy.

The cause of disunity in the body is not that the members differ from one another. That is an essential element in a living body. It arises when the members despise one another and deny their need of each other. But to take steps towards goodwill and unity demands courage, and the faith that in the Child born on Christmas Day is to be found the solvent of all human divisions. In Christ there are no longer East and West, white and black, Catholic and non-Catholic, employer and employed, male and female. All are one because in each is Christ.

Before leaving this subject of Christian unity, I want to make a further plea for a positive attitude to Christian and Quaker diversity. There is so much variety in the great family of the Christian church, and so much in that little part of it called the Society of Friends, that we have to come to terms with it and know how to react to those whose experience finds expression in ways so different from our own.

Ernest Ludlam used to enjoy telling the story of two men looking at the glory of a sunset sky. One fell on his knees in prayerful thanksgiving, while the other exclaimed, "Well, I'm damned!" Ernest Ludlam's penetrating comment was that the religion was the same, the ritual was different.

Another illustration will make my point even clearer. One day during the war, when my wife and I were caretakers of the Friends' Meeting House in Cardiff, I went to answer the front door bell. On the step was a little elderly lady, her arms splayed out from her sides because in each hand was a collection of parcels and bags. She looked up at me and asked for me by name. When I assured her that I was I, she said she had a letter for me, and looked down in perplexity at her multiplicity of baggage, wondering how to extract it; and before I could say "Come in", she dropped everything and stood in the midst of it all while she extracted a grubby envelope from a somewhat shabby handbag. She handed this to me. It was a brief note from a London Citizens' Advice Bureau saying simply, "This is to introduce Mary Ann Daly who has lost everything in the blitz. Can you help her, please?" I looked up from the word "everything" to see the little woman surrounded by paper parcels, and smiled involuntarily. She smiled too, and together we gathered up the baggage and I took her into the library where there was a fire and a comfortable chair; and there I left her while I went to get her a meal before we should talk about her future. When I returned, tray in hand, I stopped as I pushed open the door. She was standing in reverent, wrapped attention, gazing up at the picture over the fireplace. It was a picture well known to most Friends, Doyle Penrose's "The Presence in the Midst", showing the figure of Christ amid a group of Quaker worshippers. After a pause, I gently made myself known, and she very slowly turned round to face me.

"Is *that* how the Quakers worship?"

"Yes."

"*That's* what we know in the Mass."

The religion was the same, the ritual was different. "The unity of Christians . . . is already here . . . All those who love our Lord Jesus Christ . . . know this inner unity, whatever diversities there may be . . ." This, and this only, is the true basis of Christian unity.

# IV

# FRIENDS AND THE WORLD RELIGIONS

I⟙ is clear that emphasis on that of God in *every* man
leads us to consider not only the question of our relation
to those Christians who are not Friends, but also the
question of our relation to those men and women who
do not accept the Christian faith. This is a vast field, and
I have neither experience of, nor knowledge about, the
non-Christian faiths to justify my entering it. All I can do
is to peep over the hedge, and tell you what I see from
my Quaker standpoint, and, more particularly, what
that standpoint is.

Starting again from the three emphases I have chosen,
the *universality* of religious *experience* points clearly to close
relationships between all men at a deep level, but insofar
as this experience has been seen in terms of *Christian*
loyalty, this is obviously a stumbling block on the road
to unity. Let us look first at Quaker universalism.

We have already noted that it is a fundamental part
of Quaker testimony that God's light shines in the heart
of everyone, and that in fact nearly all the characteristics of Friends stem from this conviction; and although
nowadays most Christians would agree, it remains true
that no other church takes it so seriously as we do. It is
likely, therefore, that it will considerably influence our
attitude to those who do not share the Christian faith.

That this was so even in the early days of our history
is evident. Robert Barclay, writing of the universal

church which "hath been in all generations", says that it is composed of all who "become obedient to the holy light and testimony of God in their hearts, so as to become sanctified by it, and cleansed from the evils of their ways". He continues with the great assertion, "There may be members therefore of this catholic church both among heathens, Turks, Jews and all the several sorts of Christians . . . who though blinded in some things in their understanding . . . yet being upright in their hearts before the Lord . . . are . . . secretly united to God."[1]

There could hardly be a better statement of Quaker universalism. But Barclay continues to give an equally clear and emphatic statement of what has been called the Particularist trend within the Society,[2] and it is noteworthy that he regards both these as correctly belonging together, and in no sense to be separated and opposed one to another. He says,

> To be a member of a particular church of Christ, as this inward work is indispensably necessary, so is also the outward profession of, and belief in, Jesus Christ, and those holy truths delivered by his spirit in the

[1] Robert Barclay, *Apology*, 1678, X. 2. A parallel statement of Quaker universalism expressed in the evangelical language of the mid-nineteenth century, is found in J. J. Gurney's Declaration of Faith:

"The influence of the Holy Spirit is very far from being confined to those who have a knowledge of Holy Writ, and of the incarnate, crucified and risen Saviour of whom it testifies. On the contrary, it is my firm conviction that as Christ died for all men, so all men, through his mediation and sacrifice on the cross, are placed in a capacity for salvation, and receive a measure of divine light . . . so that those who believe in it, and obey it, are thereby led to fear God, and to keep his law as it is written on their hearts; . . . and thus sharing in the benefit of his atoning death on the cross, through faith in the degree of light bestowed upon them, they are to be regarded as partakers, in their measure, and according to their capacity, of the body and blood of our Lord and Saviour Jesus Christ."

*Memoirs of Joseph John Gurney*, ed. J. B. Braithwaite, 1854, II. pp. 537-8.

[2] Albert Fowler, *Two Trends in Modern Quaker Thought*, 1961.

scriptures . . . Hence it follows that the inward work of holiness, and forsaking iniquity, is necessary in every respect to the being a member in the church of Christ; and that the outward profession is necessary to be a member of a particular gathered church, but not to the being a member of the catholic church; yet it is absolutely necessary, where God affords the opportunity of knowing it; and the outward testimony is to be believed where it is presented and revealed.[1]

Because Barclay said something is, in itself, no reason for us to believe it today. But I have quoted him because I believe he says here something which does reflect accurately the belief of Friends, not only as it was, but as it is today. If I try to re-express this in my own language as my own personal conviction, it comes down to this: I know that all men everywhere know something of the promptings of love and truth in their hearts which are the leadings of God. Insofar as they are trying to be obedient to these, they may be considered to be in the invisible church, the non-institutional church, whether or not they have knowledge of the historic Jesus. But membership in the Society of Friends involves commitment in loyalty to the one God who is revealed to us supremely in Jesus Christ, and before anyone is accepted into membership of the Society, it is necessary to find out whether he wants to be "a humble learner in the school of Christ". If, having encountered Christ, he rejects him as unworthy of his reverence and loyalty, then the character of the God he worships is different from the character of the God we worship, and he would be out of place in the Society of Friends, whose purpose

[1] Robert Barclay, *Apology*, 1678, X. 4.

is to encourage discipleship of Jesus, and worship of "the God and father of our Lord Jesus Christ".

Universalism and Particularism belong together, and must remain inseparable. Each without the other is mutilated and unsatisfying. The one can be so wide and comprehensive as to be vague and meaningless with no cutting edge of purpose or loyalty; the other can be so narrow and rigid as to be a denial of Christian conviction.

E. L. Allen well says that we have to choose between two interpretations of Christianity which he terms exclusive and inclusive.

> For the first, the revelation of God in Christ is confined to a single stream of history, that which rises in Israel. For the second, what is revealed in Israel and in Christ is a dealing of God in mercy with all men at all times. The crucial significance of Christ is maintained on either view, but in the second case he is the point at which God so discloses himself that it can be seen that he is present at every point.[1]

Friends clearly choose the inclusive interpretation, and gladly recognize that this derives from the unique revelation of God given in Christ.

In this connection it may be right to say a word in passing about the perplexing text, "No man cometh unto the Father but by me" (John 14. 6). This can appear so contrary to the univeralism of which I have been speaking that it is used to deny it. I do not know what "the scholars" say about this, nor whether they are united as to the saying's authenticity and meaning. But it seems to me to mean, quite simply, that no man comes to know God, the Father, the one whose character is made manifest so clearly in Jesus, except through the Christ

[1] E. L. Allen, *Christianity among the Religions*, 1960, p. 119.

spirit at work in his heart. If he is fortunate enough to know of the historic Jesus, his knowledge of God will be so much the greater and truer; but if he knows God only by the inward light, uninformed by the historic Jesus, he still most truly knows him. If this be true, this text, far from being an exclusively particularist one, is affirming the universality of Christ: every man, whoever he is, who comes to the Father, does so through the Christ spirit at work in him.

This kind of Christian universalism which is so fundamental to the Quaker attitude to other faiths, is freshly expressed by our Friend Yukio Irie, who came to Quakerism from Buddhism.

> As for me, Jesus is a man so great that you may call him the only begotten Son of God, or Divine. We may call His Spirit Love, Light, Truth or Way. Yet that Spirit is so universal and eternal, that I cannot but believe that it has been prevailing everywhere, more or less in all religions, even from before the birth of the historic Jesus, and I believe that it is living more or less in all human beings in the world. This is why Jesus says all that he has taught us is our Father's and not Jesus' own.[1]

Such is the standpoint from which I look at the non-Christian faiths, or, more accurately, at the individuals who belong to them. What does this imply in terms of relationship?

It implies, first, a real respect for the faith of others. Friends are trained in their business meetings to seek for the will of God through the experience and judgement of others. If one is believed to speak under guidance, it behoves all to listen under guidance. If there really is

[1] *Sharing Our Quaker Faith*, ed. E. B. Bronner, 1959, p. 123.

that of God in every man, then every man may be a channel through whom God may be better known to us and this is true for those of other faiths as well as for fellow Friends and fellow Christians, though the form of their thought and experience may be less familiar to us.

Closely linked with this, there is the assurance that there is common ground between all men of faith. The extent of this may vary according to many circumstances, but if there is that of God in every man, there must be something in common in all men's faith.

If this be so, there must be opportunity for mutual learning through sharing the insights which faith has given. Sometimes we may be able to share the wonder of Christ with one who has not known him, or has only met him so clothed in dogma that he was unable to recognize him for what he is. And sometimes we may be able to learn more of what he is, and what our response to him should be, through the eyes of those who have not felt it right to join the institutional Christian church. As I was thinking about this, a Hindu student called Padmabai gave an address in Woodbrooke on The Cross which all who heard it felt had illuminated for them a mystery which will always be unfathomable. All the Christians were indebted to the Hindu for the deepening of their understanding through the depth of her insight.[1] Or, to take another simple example, I still remember a Hindu student at Cambridge talking to the Cambridge University Friends' Society (as it then was) on a Hindu's view of Christianity, and the shame we all felt when, having asked quietly, "Do you really believe in the Sermon on the Mount, or do you think it is just poetry?" he added quietly, "I believe it." We so-called Christians

[1] This was printed in the *Woodbrooke International Journal*, June 1961.

learned something of loyalty to Christ in his simple and profound affirmation.

Such thinking leads to a certain blurring of boundaries, a recognition that labels are often much more divisive than they should be, and that unity of faith is found where faith unites rather than in sharing an outward name. We do well to be suspicious of exaggerated difference between highly abstract statements about this faith and that.

But so far I have spoken of what we see from the universal side of our faith, and it is necessary to put alongside this the claims of Christian loyalty, the particularity of Christ, remembering that both equally belong to our Quaker faith. This does not go contrary to anything I have said, but gives it point and purpose, and saves the universalism from becoming so wide and comprehensive as to be quite meaningless.

The report of the study groups on "What is our Faith?" at the last world conference of Friends, puts clearly the claim of the universal and the particular.

> The Quaker faith is Christian. This involves a belief that all people everywhere are within the family of God who is our Father. God has been apprehended in other religions and we feel in fellowship with all who truly seek Him . . . God has revealed Himself in many ways but the supreme revelation of His love comes to man through Christ upon the cross . . . The root and ground of our experience and therefore of our common belief must be the revelation of God in Christ. God expressed His love historically in Jesus of Nazareth, and eternally through the Spirit of Christ. What Jesus was like in history—in His life, teaching, death and resurrection—God is like in eternity.[1]

[1] *Friends Face their Fourth Century*, 1952, pp. 41-42.

If this is a characteristic statement of Quaker faith, as I believe it is, it is clear that we do not believe that all faiths are equally true and equally adequate to meet the needs of their adherents. It means that while we accept gladly the fact that there is truth in all faiths, we believe that in Jesus Christ the nature of God was supremely revealed, and that a true understanding of him takes us nearer to a true understanding of God than do the insights of any other faith. It means that as Friends we gladly re-affirm, "The Quaker faith is Christian". It means that in inter-faith worshipping groups we shall make clear that the character of the God whom we worship is Christlike. It means that those who seek membership in the Society of Friends should know that "the root and ground of our experience and therefore of our common belief must be the revelation of God in Christ". It means that when we speak of the light that lighteth every man that cometh into the world, or that of God in every man, we are referring to the Christ spirit.

Friends, therefore, cannot favour syncretism if it means an attempt to sink differences in order to achieve union. We would expect that as men come more faithfully to follow the light, they will be led to ever deeper and fuller understanding of its nature as being in line with the character of Christ. This may mean sloughing off much of the accretion which has accumulated around him and obscured him, and both Western and Eastern religious experience may well help each other in this deeper, truer apprehension of the character of God.

E. L. Allen sums this up excellently:

> The Christian can enter into conversation with men and women of another faith because his aim in this is not to

win them for his religion, but to serve that Kingdom of
Christ whose triumphs are only those of truth and love.
He is willing to receive into the fellowship of the church
all who would confess Christ by name; indeed, he
invites them to enter it. But he does not demand that all
become Christians. For he knows that Christendom has
so sadly misinterpreted Christ that he may draw some
to himself within their own religions as he could not do
by gaining them for ours.[1]

We may think of Christianity in relation to the other
great world faiths in one of several different ways. We
may think of it as the one only true faith. We may think
of it as one among several each of which is more or less
equally valid, and which severally appeal to different
groups of people. Or we may think of it as one of several
faiths, each of which possesses its own validity, but we
would claim that Christianity comes nearer than any of
the others to an understanding of the ultimate nature of
reality. For myself, I think of Christianity in this last
way. This is well expressed in the Study-in-Fellowship
pamphlet, *Worship and Witness* (1961, p. 2):

> The revelation of the nature of God . . . which has come
> to us through Jesus Christ is the most fruitful because it
> is the most completely possessed of truth of any that has
> been given to the human race. This implies a rejection
> of the attitude which would have us consider Christi-
> anity simply as one belief among many; it carries with it
> an assertion that a true Christian belief leads to a deeper
> insight into the meaning of life than Hindu, Buddhist or
> humanist beliefs.

[1] E. L. Allen, *Christianity among the Religions*, 1960, p. 155.

# V

# IS QUAKERISM FOR THE MANY
# OR THE FEW?

EMPHASIS on *every man's experience* of *Christ* leads naturally
to asking the question, Is Quakerism for the many or the
few? In answering this it is natural to look at Quakerism
within Christianity in the same way as we have just
looked at Christianity among the world religions,
because it is, quite simply, our understanding of
Christianity. Do we think of it as the one only true faith?
Or do we think of it as one among several understand-
ings of Christianity each of which is more or less equally
valid and which appeal to different kinds of people? Or
do we think of it as one of the many branches of the
Christian church, each of which possesses its own validity
and special emphasis, but none of which so nearly
understands the nature of true Christianity?

My impression is that very few Friends would claim
that Quakerism is the one only true faith;[1] but I believe

[1] There is a striking difference between the present and the seventeenth century attitude in this respect, noted a century ago by Thomas
Hancock: "In 1658 there was not a Quaker living who did not believe
Quakerism to be the one only true Church of the living God. In 1858
there is not a Quaker living who does believe it." (*The Peculium*, 1859,
p. 8.) But Thomas Hancock overstates the position, at least for
1658. There is, for example, the well-known passage from Isaac
Penington's examination of the grounds of religious persecution in New
England where Quakers were facing the death penalty, a book first
published in 1659: "and oh, how sweet and pleasant it is to the truly
spiritual eye to see several sorts of believers, several forms of Christians in
the school of Christ, every one learning their own lesson, performing their
own peculiar service, and knowing, owning and loving one another in
their several places and different performances to their Master, to whom
they are to give an account, and not to quarrel with one another about

many Friends could be found to support each of the other two positions. It is necessary to examine these a little more carefully if we are to see at all clearly what is the answer to the question, Is Quakerism for the many or the few? If Quakerism is merely one of many more or less equally valid interpretations of Christianity, it is bound forever to represent but a small fragment of the whole Christian church; whereas if it is thought of as the interpretation which most nearly approximates to truth, we may hope that, if we are faithful in proclaiming it in life and word, men will increasingly respond to it. This does not necessarily imply that all Christians will join the Society of Friends, but rather that other branches of the church will accept more of Quaker insight into their systems. And, lest I seem to claim too much for Friends, let me quote with approval a remark of Zebedee Haines, a beloved American Friend of a century ago. Asked by his small son, "In heaven, will there be anybody besides Friends?" he replied, "Well, Roger, if there's not, I guess it will hardly be worth while keeping the place open."

My own position on this question can be summarized briefly and crudely in four propositions:

---

their different practices. (Rom. 14.4). For this is the true ground of love and unity, not that such a man walks and does just as I do, but because I feel the same Spirit and life in him, and that he walks in his rank, in his own order, in his proper way and place of subjection to that; and this is far more pleasing to me than if he walked just in that track wherein I walk. Nay, so far as I am spiritual, I cannot so much as desire that he should do so, until he be particularly led thereto, by the same Spirit which led me . . . The way is one; Christ the truth of God; and he that is in the faith, and in the obedience to that light which shines from his Spirit into the heart of every believer, hath a taste of the one heart and of the one way, and knoweth that no variety of practices, which is of God, can make a breach in the true unity." (Quoted from *Christian Faith and Practice in the Experience of the Society of Friends*, 1960, 222.)

1. That Christianity is the most completely possessed of truth of any of the world's faiths, and that Quakerism is the most completely possessed of truth of any of the church's branches;
2. that therefore we should be committed to a greater faith in the truth of which we are convinced, and unashamedly proclaim it as the truth;
3. that until we do this we shall inevitably be for the few, and when we do it we shall be for the many more;
4. but that, men being what they are, committed Christians will in each generation be in the position of a remnant in tension with the world, a leaven in the larger lump.

I have deliberately put this crudely, without the qualifications and explanations or even apology that it calls for, in order to show clearly the direction in which I am asking you to look. And at once there must be strong criticism. Two charges in particular must be faced: gross arrogance, and gross unrealism.

When we look at the saintly men and women of the rest of the Christian church; when we look at the splendid work done by all the different denominations; when we think of our own tinyness in that great company —how can I be so crassly arrogant as to claim that the Quaker understanding of Christianity is the truest? But note: I am not claiming that Friends are in any way better than other Christians; I am claiming that their belief is a truer understanding of God and particularly man's relationship to him and to his fellow men. I am not claiming that our present understanding is complete or final; I am claiming that in its incomplete, present form it is nearest to understanding the nature of reality. Nor am I claiming that we have nothing to learn from other traditions whose insights do in fact so much enrich our own understanding, and could do so much more if we would open ourselves more fully to their influence.

But, having said all this, let us ask, Why is the convinced Friend a Friend?[1] Surely for the same reason that a Buddhist is a Buddhist, a Christian is a Christian, a Methodist is a Methodist—because, in each case, he believes that that form and fellowship of faith and practice is the one most completely possessed of truth. If we do not believe this of our particular religion, surely we are in the wrong place. If we believe that Methodism is truer than Quakerism, or Buddhism truer than Christianity, we are in the wrong group (unless we are deliberately seeking to convert from inside by a kind of fifth column activity). So it seems to me that there is no more arrogance involved than there is in any other religious commitment. We are here concerned with our understanding of truth, and not with matters of preference, taste, temperament, etc.

The charge of gross unrealism is certainly formidable. After three centuries there are 200,000 Friends in a world population of about 3,000 million—one one hundred and fiftieth per cent. In our own country there are 21,000 in a population of over fifty million. Among the other Christian churches we are the smallest of the better known denominations. Quakerism seems clearly enough to be for the few, and the very, very few at that.

But it is not only numbers which cry out that we are for the few. There are many, even among Friends, who believe that we are only for particular categories of

[1] I am here concerned only with conscious religious commitment, and not with social, hereditary, geographical and other reasons for membership.

people. When one asks what categories, it is less easy to find a clear answer. Some say that Friends only appeal to the well educated, some to the thoughtful, some to those who are individualistic and at home in minority positions but not to those whose temperaments lead them to the anonymity of conformity. Some think that Friends can only appeal to those who are willing to take responsibility, and initiative, but not to those whose nature is passive and receptive who would never be so well nourished in a Friends' Meeting for Worship as in a liturgical service or one in which a meaty sermon was the heart of the sandwich.

At first glance there seems likely to be some truth in this line of thought, especially if one takes a rather superficial look at the Friends of today who most regularly attend our Meetings for Worship and Church Affairs. But if one looks at this historically, and even if one goes through any list of members and tries to visualize each one as they are at 11.0 a.m. on Mondays, as well as at that time on Sundays, then the picture we have sketched becomes very unconvincing.

Look for example at the social background and temperamental variety of the first generation of Friends, and see what a wonderful range there was. George Fox with rough speech and highly original spelling, and Isaac Penington a cultured scholarly saint; Margaret Fell the gracious lady of Swarthmore Hall, and Mary Fisher the servant girl; Samuel Fisher the well-trained theologian, and James Nayler the "plain simple husbandman"; and so on. What common factor of temperament, social background or education united these into one close fellowship? Or if we pick out a few of the best-known Friends from every period—George

Fox, William Penn, John Woolman, Elizabeth Fry—what is common among them apart from their Quaker faith? Or if we hear it said that English Quakers at present are mostly drawn from those with more education, do we remember that it was John Wilhelm Rowntree who lamented only two generations ago that while the Society of Friends could successfully appeal to humble working men, it seemed unable to reach the more educated?[1]

This kind of thing is suggestive: it makes one look again at the facts, and makes me ask whether the generalizations that I have quoted are true. As I examine them, I find they are very little supported by evidence.

The commonest is that Friends cannot appeal to the less educated, whereas the truth seems to be that in this generation we do not—which is quite different. When John Wilhelm Rowntree wrote, Friends were in intimate, personal regular contact with thousands of illiterate men and women through the adult school movement, and the result was that men and women were attracted into the Society in quite large numbers. At the same period, Friends were not in any comparable way in touch with the more educated part of British society. Since then, what has happened? Two things. On the one hand, Friends have largely withdrawn from the adult school movement which itself has changed its character in response to changes in our educational system. On the other, Friends' stress on the importance of secondary education has given the children of all members the opportunity which many of their parents had not, and there is in every generation an educational levelling up. With what result? Until 1944 the adults of

[1] *Proceedings of the Manchester Conference*, 1895, p. 80.

this country could be divided into those who left school at fourteen and those who had longer schooling, and this division ran right through the whole of life. It determined the jobs they did, the games they played, the books and papers they read (if any), the radio programmes to which they listened, the films they chose to watch. Broadly speaking, unless there was some special reason for it, there was functional, but no effective personal, contact between the two groups. And if there was no personal contact, there could be no effective communication.

What conclusions can we draw from this? First, that it is not Quakerism which fails to appeal, but Quakers who fail to bridge the gap; the fault lies not in our faith, dear Friends, but in ourselves. As Thomas Green reminded us in his Swarthmore Lecture, "Our failures are due to the spiritual mediocrity of which most of us are guilty, and not to the inadequacy of Quakerism to meet the needs of men."[1] And second, that if we can find a way of making effective, personal contact, and if we really have faith in our faith and can proclaim it with conviction, we are likely to find a thankful response. The univeral element in Quaker faith gives us confidence that we have a message for every one.

There is no need to expand the first conclusion: each one of us must realize our "spiritual mediocrity" and the lukewarmth of much of our faith and practice, and must face the challenge personally. But the second conclusion deserves emphasis. It seems to me that our freedom from precisely defined dogma gives us special opportunity, and therefore special responsibility, to meet people for whom the precepts and practices of much institutional

[1] T. F. Green, *Preparation for Worship*, 1952, p. 2.

religion are unacceptable. We can and must meet men where they are, finding and answering that of God in them, showing them that we are fellow seekers, but being willing to share that which we have already found since we are not only seekers but finders. This means that we must be honest with ourselves about what we have found, and make the effort of will and mental discipline to formulate it to ourselves which must precede any communication to others. But the manner and content of such communication must vary as we are "all things to all men". As we seek to meet men where they actually are, we find that there is much common ground. We can go to every one with the opening phrases of the General Advices, whether he be theist, agnostic or atheist: "Take heed, dear Friends, to the promptings of love and truth in your hearts . . ." Every one knows these promptings, and from there we can go on to share where "heeding" them has taken us in our search for Ultimate Reality, call it what we will. And it takes us, as the rest of that first paragraph so beautifully and simply says, to Jesus Christ, the Way, the Truth, the Life, though we may mediate this in language suited to our hearer.[1]

There is not space here to expand the argument, or to examine the many questions which arise. It must suffice to introduce two examples. The first is an account, published in *Wayfarer* of March, 1961, but probably still essentially true, of an African Meeting for Worship. This

[1] "Take heed, dear Friends, to the promptings of love and truth in your hearts, which are the leadings of the Holy Spirit of God. Resist not his strivings within you. It is his light that shows us our darkness and leads to true repentance. It is God's love that draws us to him, a redemptive love shown forth in Jesus Christ in all his life and above all on the cross. He is the Way, the Truth and the Life."

I do the more gladly since another generalization is often made which so far I have not quoted. But you will have heard it said, "Your Quaker Meetings may be all right for the Englishman who is quiet and restrained and thoughtful, but what about the Welshman who wants to let himself go in singing hymns, or the African whose religious life is bound up with rhythm and sound?" Barbara Acquah, describing Hill House Meeting in Achimota, Ghana, wrote:

> Its manner of worship is in no way different from that of Meetings in England, although half of its attendance is African and half is drawn from three other continents ... It is a good example of that diversity in unity which characterizes Friends' Meetings at their best. In its variety of beliefs it is like a many coloured cloth, carefully hand-woven, and of such a complex pattern that every newcomer finds himself a part of it, contributing his own peculiar (sometimes startling) brightness to the artistry of the whole. Those who participate in our study group with such keenness and humour range from the scientific philosopher contemplating research into the nature of an impersonal God, to the ardent fundamentalist claiming personal salvation from a divine act of sacrifice. They puzzle each other, no doubt, but there is a winsome frankness in the atmosphere which helps them to accept each other's position and "keep their minds open to new truth from whatever quarter it may arise".
>
> ... Recently a suggestion was brought to Elders' meeting that some of our Attenders might find silent Meeting uncongenial, and prefer a little hymn-singing, not during Meeting, but perhaps instead of our study group, or at our informal gatherings after Meeting. We could not, however, find any enthusiasm for introducing such practice.

The other example is a comment on those who say that our way of worship is all right for the well educated and sophisticated whose minds are filled with suitable material on which to meditate, but not for those without this equipment. It concerns a well-known youth club in Birmingham which caters for teenagers on a typical modern suburban housing estate. At the end of the lively, noisy Sunday evening programme, these twelve to eighteen year olds come, if they like, to a silent half hour together. The leader tells them that if they know what prayer is, they can pray; if they don't, they are to think as positively as they can about the people they meet, the work they do, the kind of person they want to be. If any member would like the group to think of anyone in special need, this is mentioned at the beginning, but otherwise there is unbroken silence. Nearly all these youngsters freely join this silent activity. One teddy-boyish lad who had recently joined the club and found himself mixed up in this unusual context, commented to the leader, "Queer this business, ain't it? Sort of *cleanses* yer, don't it?"—which in modern Birmingham jargon surely paraphrases the familiar words of the cultured Robert Barclay written three centuries ago:

> When I came into the silent assemblies of God's people, I felt a secret power among them, which touched my heart, and as I gave way unto it, I found the evil weakening in me, and the good raised up . . .[1]

My contention is that Quakerism is for the few because we are failing to communicate it to the many, but that there is nothing in Quakerism which makes it necessarily for the few. I believe that as long as we are lukewarm,

[1] Robert Barclay, *Apology*, 1678, Prop. XI. 7.

believing with part of our minds in part of our faith and practice, we shall never succeed in sharing it with others. Faith involves wholehearted surrender of the whole person, and it is only that kind of commitment which can be infectious and kindle faith in another heart. But if we believe without arrogance that Christianity is the most completely possessed of truth of any of the world's religions, and that Quakerism is the most completely possessed of truth of any of the Christian denominations, then we should go forth in faith to proclaim that which we know. The ringing challenge of the first Swarthmore Lecture deserves to be repeated:

> Let us stop assuming that the great days of Quakerism were in the seventeenth century, and that we are a tiny remnant left behind to chronicle the story of spent fires and dead issues. The great days of Quakerism are to be in the twentieth century . . . The momentous question is, shall we quit ourselves like men and do, in the high spirit of early Friends, the work of this age.[1]

It is not irrelevant to the thought of this section, to introduce a quaint extract from the writings of Joseph John Gurney, written at the time when Quakerism in England was most obviously for the few and a dwindling few, but this did not cloud his vision of the universality of the truths that Friends were seeking to embody, which looked truer in the light of eternity than in the social milieu of early nineteenth-century England.

> When we are favoured to arrive on the heavenly shores, shall we not find an innumerable host of *true Quakers?* Will there be any worshippers there in the letter and not in the life? Any prayers and praises uttered out of

[1] Rufus M. Jones, *Quakerism, A Religion of Life*, 1908, pp. 43-44.

the immediate influence of the Holy Spirit? Any ceremonial observances? Any oaths? Any compliments? Any war? A broad negation meets every one of these questions.[1]

[1] *Memoirs of Joseph John Gurney*, 1854, I. pp. 233-234.

# WHAT THINK WE OF CHRIST?

NEAR the beginning of this lecture, I suggested that two of the characteristics of that of God in every man are that this is known in experience, i.e. to the whole man, and that it is experience of Christ. I have also several times suggested that there is, and must be, diversity of approach to him, and that this is something to be welcomed and faced frankly, not as an embarrassment but as a source of strength.

In this last section I want to look a little more closely at the diversity of approach to Christ which is characteristic of Friends today, and which has appeared in various forms during our history. Most Friends will be aware of the commoner forms of expressing this in controversial terms, in which pairs of factors are picked out and put in contrast one to another: the historic and the inward, the orthodox and the liberal, the Evangelical and the Hicksite, the trinitarian and the unitarian, the particularist and the universalist.

My contention is that these are not rightly seen in opposition one to another as alternatives, but that they represent complementary aspects of one reality; that they are not to be thought of as different conclusions, but as different starting points. If we believe this, in discussion we shall not allow ourselves to be forced back into defensive arrogance in which our prejudices become more fixed, but we shall have open minds in which we are ready to discover more of an aspect of truth that has so far meant little or nothing to us.

It is a further contention that this approach springs straight out of essential Quakerism. If at the heart of Quaker conviction lies the affirmation that the Light of Christ is known in measure to every man, we can neither expect nor desire that every man will formulate his experience in exactly the same way. Jesus is too great for any formula adequately to express his significance, and his greatness will appear differently to different people. It is not the particular facet of greatness that appeals to one and another which is significant; it is Jesus himself who is significant. "From scheme and creed the light goes out . . . ; the blessed Master none can doubt." "The heart of so great a mystery cannot ever be reached by following one road only." We are all "humble learners in the school of Christ".[1]

This last inspired phrase, which I believe we owe to Edward Grubb, brings in another important fact. A humble  learner is not one who has arrived, but is "open to new light from whatever quarter it may arise".[2] He is one whose understanding and experience yesterday was different from that of today, and may be different again tomorrow. This does not mean that he is swept hither and thither without anchorage, but that his experience of the subject of his study is constantly enlarging. It behoves each one of us to try to understand more deeply that which is precious and significant in other people's discovery of Christ, if our own is to be as full as possible.

With this in mind, and remembering that I have been asked to be personal, I propose now to try to state something of my own approach to Christ, not because I think

[1] *Church Government*, 1931, III. para. 16.
[2] The 12th Query.

it is of particular interest as being mine, still less because I think it is the one, only, true approach. Rather I do so because I know that very many within the Society think along lines somewhat similar to these, and they are much less frequently articulate than the more orthodox whose position is naturally expressed in the corporate statements of the Society and the abundant writings of theologians.

Reverting to my simile of the spectrum, if the corporate expression of the Society's belief about Christ is in the centre, I am aware that my own position lies left of centre. I am aware, too, that this is partly determined by the period in which I grew to maturity, and that another generation is stressing other facets of faith than those which are most alive for me. But, as I have been trying to say, we both need each other's insights.

Like many others growing up in the interwar period, especially among those whose training was in science, I went through, and in many respects remain in, an attitude of reverent agnosticism. Thomas Henry Huxley's account of how he coined the word appealed to me. You remember how he found himself among a group of distinguished people who each seemed to know clearly where he stood, and adopted a label usually ending in -ic or -ist. Huxley did not fit into any of the known categories, and he tells us how he felt like a fox without a tail. He could not accept dogmatic statements of supposed truth unless there were evidence to prove them, and atheist, theist and pantheist each seemed impossible on this basis. Thinking like this, he coined the word "agnostic" in contrast to the "gnostic" who made such categorical assertions about the nature of existence without a shadow of evidence to support them. He was an agnostic, open minded and ready to receive new light from whatever quarter it might come, but unwilling to dogmatize about that which he could not prove. And so, with a tail to wave, he took his place among his "normally elongated companions" with more satisfaction.[1]

This seemed to me wholly satisfactory, until I began to realize that in fact we do have faith in all sorts of things without being able to prove them. We take things on trust, in faith. We *know* the love of parents without being able to prove it. Faith is in a very real sense evidence of things not seen, not proved or provable. Agnosticism and faith must go hand in hand, in fruitful tension one with another, checking the traditional statements and thought-forms of Christianity, inherited from a pre-Darwinian naïve faith in revealed religion, and leaving room for the vital, vitalizing faith growing out of inner conviction and insight in which rational thought is but one factor.

At this time, in my late teens, I had the opportunity of a talk with C. F. Andrews to whom I unfolded some of my perplexity about religion in general and Christianity in particular. Thinking as I have indicated, I could accept the reality and ultimacy of love, and affirm with certainty that God is love; but to affirm that God is a loving father was impossible. I also knew that love required from me a disciplined response in commitment, and knew dimly that this was truly a "response" to something which seemed "outside" me, but I could not honestly think in terms like the "will" and "purpose" of God. As nearly the whole of Christian thought was

[1] Essay on *Agnosticism*, 1889.

expressed in these personal terms, it seemed to me meaningless and anthropomorphic to the point of being credulous and superstitious, and consequently most off-putting. This made prayer impossible, for prayer seemed to pre-suppose a person to whom to pray. C. F. Andrews listened sympathetically, and then said something like this: To me three words are almost interchangeable: God, Christ and Love. Sometimes I think of God as God the Father and Creator; sometimes I think of him as made personal in Jesus; sometimes I think of him as Love. If only one of these means anything real to you, hold on to it firmly, and gradually you will come to find meaning in the others. And meanwhile, when you come across people saying and writing things about God and Christ, translate, as far as you can, into Love, and see if it makes more sense. As for prayer, sometimes I pray to God the Father; sometimes I imagine that I am talking with Jesus and I try to think what he would say to me (here he interrupted with a twinkle to say that this is very dangerous as we may too easily put into Jesus' mouth the words we would like him to say to us); and sometimes I just ask myself, "What does Love require of me in this situation?"

His advice bore wonderful fruit. Ministry in Meetings was transformed from nonsense to sense (usually!). Much that I had dismissed became real and relevant, and before long Jesus ceased to be a legendary man-God and came to be seen as the supreme embodiment in history of Love: particular, real, relevant, and, somehow, strangely contemporary. He became both really historic, and also leapt from history into the present, so that the presentness of his spirit alive and at work in the world, was a great, dependable reality. And this aliveness made some sense, and increasingly more sense, of the resurrection. The phrase "the risen Christ" came to be meaningful and usable, whereas "the risen Socrates" did not. As C. F. Andrews had predicted, Jesus came to mean ever more and more, to grow in significance both as the historic Jesus of Nazareth, and as the contemporary Christ known personally and through this experience of relationship, the analogy of personality in relation to God came to be more understandable and eventually acceptable as the most adequate way of expressing this vital, personal experience; but it remains an analogy, and to forget this leads straight into dangerous anthropomorphism which erects a formidable barrier between those within and those outside the churches.

There is no need to develop this theme. Enough has been said to show the way my religious experience grew. Many problems remained, and many still are the questions to which I reply with reverent agnosticism, "I do not know"; and I am content to leave them unanswered rather than strain faith by the acceptance of thought-forms which cannot be quite sincerely mine.

This approach to Jesus is, of course, seeing him first as son of man, and only later accepting him as in some sense son of God. How do I understand the divinity and humanity of Jesus? What do I make of the doctrine of the Trinity?

If we try to imagine ourselves in the position of the first disciples, we would have to think of ourselves as strictly monotheistic Jews, believing in the one God, Jehovah, the creator. As they associated with Jesus, they gradually came to recognize more and more in him: first the special rabbi who taught with authority and not as the scribes; then the Christ, the holy one of God; finally

74

the affirmation of Thomas, "My Lord and my God". What a terribly shocking thing for a Jew to have said— and yet, somehow, that was the effect of the impact Jesus made. And then, after his earthly life was finished, these same disciples and their friends were aware of the continuing life of his spirit among them, encouraging, guiding and sustaining them. In short, they had a threefold experience of one reality: they knew God the father; they knew the person of Jesus who was so identified with him that Thomas could burst out with his great affirmation; and they knew the continuing inspiration of the spirit which they identified with him. The same threefold experience has been possible to those who did not know Jesus in his earthly life, from Paul down to ourselves. Our experience of God is essentially threefold, and as essentially one. We know him as God; we know him personified in Jesus; we know him as the spirit of love and truth in our hearts; and each of these is a way of experiencing the one same ultimate reality.

This is as far as my faith takes me in this direction. I realize that the complexities of translation through Greek and Latin to English have in part been responsible for thinking in terms of three persons, and that meta-physicians have pushed this still further in claiming that there must be society in the godhead, because, if God is love, there must be lover and beloved. All this leaves me cold, being an example of what I spoke of earlier of the danger of theological statements being two or three removes from experience.[1] As long as our trinitarian thinking reflects our trinitarian experience, it is useful; when it becomes a metaphysical dogma by which orthodoxy should be measured, it is seriously harmful.

[1] p. 29.

And while the emphasis is on experience of the one God known in three ways, like water being known to us as ice, water and steam, the the emphasis is on the oneness of God.

It is in the vitality of this experience of God that unity may be found. This is well put by Margaret Hobling. Referring to the tension between the trinitarian and unitarian aspects of the revelation of God in Christ, she comments,

> In the Society of Friends, the characteristic form of this tension is not the co-existence of two fully formulated rival creeds competing for adherents, but different stresses and emphases in the thinking of its members. This is only possible so long as the life of the Society, in its worship and its service, confronts them with a reality so inexhaustibly rich that these different aspects are but broken lights, and in the unity of the shared life we all learn from one another. The spiritual exchanges of the Christian life are very deep.[1]

But though we offer this link between trinitarian and unitarian, we have still to look at the person of Jesus Christ, the figure who evoked from Thomas his great affirmation of faith. In many discussions of the unitarian and trinitarian positions, the crux of the matter lies less in the unitary or threefold nature of God and more in what we mean by the divinity and humanity of Jesus.

In approaching this subject I know of no better passage than that drafted originally, I believe, by my beloved teacher and predecessor in Woodbrooke, Gerald K. Hibbert. It is part of a fine statement prepared by Yorkshire Quarterly Meeting at the time of the

[1] "Early Friends and The Doctrine of the Trinity", in *Then and Now*, ed. Anna Brinton, 1960, p. 130.

momentous revision of Part I of the Book of Discipline just after the first world war, and it has stood in that volume since 1922, being retained in the recent revision.

> The New Testament clearly sets out Christ as fully human and as fully divine. The writers are conscious of no difficulty or contradiction involved in this position. It seemed to them the most natural thing in the world. Probably the sense of contradiction only arises in our minds through ignorance of what is meant by personality. We have set divinity over against humanity, on the assumption that so much added to the one must be so much subtracted from the other. Some have so emphasized Christ's divinity as to leave no room for his humanity, while others have done just the reverse. It seems so easy to solve the problem by cutting the knot; either say that Christ was absolute God, or that he was ordinary man. But this does not solve the problem, for either solution fails to take account of many of the facts. The difficulty is to get a conception of Jesus that is true to all the facts—of one who was the Incarnate Son of God and yet (perhaps we should say "and *therefore*") was truly man. It is a pity that we insist on using the terms "humanity" and "divinity" as though they imply opposition. May we not rather say that Jesus "shows us the divine life humanly lived and the human life divinely lived"? But of one thing we can be certain, there are depths beneath depths and heights above heights in the Personality of Jesus, which make rash generalizations or superficial solutions absurd. We are standing before the greatest character in history and we may well hesitate before trying to express him in a formula.[1]

This passage was the gateway which led me from a profound faith in Jesus as son of man, to a growing

[1] *Christian Faith and Practice*, 1960, para. 157.

appreciation of Jesus as Son of God. It really recognized his manhood, his real manhood, and at the same time pointed to the way in which his stature seems to burst the bonds of manhood, to be the meeting point of divine and human. This meeting point is tremendously important: it is the col at which two routes coming from different directions, meet on their way to the summit, God. It is expressed in a duality of thought for this reason, in phrases which nonetheless try to express the oneness of the subject. Gerald Hibbert quotes the divine life humanly lived and the human life divinely lived. The International Missionary Council's conference in Jerusalem in 1928 adopted a statement on The Christian Message which said, "He is the revelation of what God is, and of what man, through him, may become."[1] J. S. Whale put it neatly in the words, "He is what God means by 'Man'. He is what man means by 'God'."[2]

Coming up the track represented by faith in the manhood of Jesus, sayings like this mean something and are acceptable, though they leave some uncertainty about the meaning of the concept "divinity". It is at this point that a thought which recurs frequently in William Temple's writings helped me. We normally think from the known to the unknown and in the nature of things we cannot know much about the content of the word "divine". When we say that Jesus is divine, says Temple, we are saying something about God rather than about Jesus. We are saying in effect, God is Christlike. The dark word God becomes filled with light, and as we contemplate the greatness of Jesus, we know that, what-

[1] Report of the Jerusalem Conference, I. p. 480.
[2] J. S. Whale, *Christian Doctrine*, 1942 ed. p.104.

ever else God may be, his character must be like that, full of grace and truth. The word was made flesh and dwelt among us.

It seems to me that most orthodox Christians come up to this col from the other side. I fear I misrepresent many, but it does seem that they start with a firm hold on God, whose character they accept on trust from the Bible, and who is consequently thought of in terms more anthropomorphic than I can accept. They see him purposing to send his beloved son, the only begotten, to redeem this sin-bound world, and as they reach the top they faintly glimpse the manhood of Jesus before the clouds envelop them. But though they try to do justice to his manhood, this emphasis on his divine nature often destroys their attempt. They recoil from such texts as "the firstborn of many brethren", "greater things than these shall ye do", or from the implications of the Jerusalem Conference statement, "He is the revelation of . . . what man, through him, may become." How can man ever become God Incarnate?

I come the other way, beginning with Jesus the carpenter's son, glimpsing something of his godliness. The one approach seems often not to give adequate room to his humanity. It stresses a supernatural birth, supernatural powers during life, supernatural resurrection and ascension, and reduces Jesus to a kind of archangel, robbing him for me of all significance and even interest. Such a one can in no sense be saviour or redeemer for me. But Jesus as a man, *really* tempted at all points like as we are, yet without sin; a man living a life so completely in harmony with God that we know as a matter of faith that God is like that—such a Jesus redeems and saves. "He is the revelation of what God is,

79

and of what man, through him, may become." This is the gospel.

Geoffrey Nuttall writes, "Nothing is gained, much is lost, if we seek to describe, or to understand, Jesus in categories which are not open to humanity, especially to humanity as deeply affected by him."[1] And another passage from Gerald Hibbert, this time from his Swarthmore Lecture of 1924, says so well what I want to say that again I must quote from him.

> If the belief in the Inner Light be true, humanity is instinct with God, and the Complete Man would be divine. At any rate, there would seem to be one principle from which we must never depart in attempting to estimate the character of Christ—nothing must be admitted which in any way lessens his full humanity. Whatever does so, lessens His value for us. If he had no genuine and developing moral experience, if He was a God masquerading in human form, if He was unable to sin or if it was easier for Him to do right than it is for us —then His life loses its validity and meaning. As long as we stand by His true manhood we are safe. We might almost say—and it is not irreverent—"Take care of His manhood, and His Godhood will take care of itself." The whole history of the Christian Church shows how difficult the Church has found it to do this. In a natural desire to do Him honour, the Church has forgotten or minimized or played tricks with His manhood, and has in so doing robbed him of His moral value.[2]

I recognize that orthodoxy and I are climbing this mountain from opposite sides. Orthodoxy seems to me to begin with a gift of faith that many within, and all

[1] G. F. Nuttall: *Better than Life. The Lovingkindness of God*, 1962, p. 65.
[2] G. K. Hibbert, *The Inner Light and Modern Thought*, 1924, pp. 62-63. Cf. also pp. 56-57.

outside, the church have not; the great majority of us begin on the other side of the mountain. I recognize that we each have much to learn as we reach the shoulder and glimpse the vista beyond. I recognize that the other route is a real and possible one for those who happen to begin on the other side, just as it is impossible for me who happens to have started on my side. And all this implies that two people may, in fact, be going in opposite directions but to the same place, and that we should be tender one with another in speaking of the validity of our findings. "We try to remember that to faithful seekers, though the roads may be many, yet the goal is one."[1] We need, in short, to be humble learners in the school of Christ, recognizing that what matters is not how far on which route we have gone, but whether we are looking in the right direction.

What matters, then, is not so much what we think about Christ, but that we think about and know him, and, still more, that we follow him.

My plea is that in the Society of Friends we recognize this, and hold on to it firmly. We need the enrichment that each can give to others from his experience of Christ. The different theological wings of the Society are not to be thought of as sharply contradictory, but as representing complementary emphases. We need the humility to believe that there is some truth in positions which we cannot accept for ourselves, and to try to discover the meaningful emphasis which they embody. But we need strict sincerity and integrity, and the recognition that what we have come to for ourselves in trying to formulate our faith, is but a stepping stone on the way to understanding a mystery which will always

[1] London Yearly Meeting, 1914, Epistle.

remain beyond embodiment in language and even in thought.

What I am trying clumsily to say, was written tersely to *The Friend* in January, 1961, by Beatrice Saxon Snell:

> In this day and age the place where Friends find their unity is in the kind of God they worship. Their apprehension of the relationship of Jesus Christ to God embraces every orthodox and unorthodox shade of theology from Unitarian to Trinitarian: but whether we regard Jesus, in whose school we are all humble learners, as God himself or as the supreme revealer of God to man, it is the same *kind* of God; a spirit of peace, truth, love and redeeming power.
>
> We need to feel the influence of this Spirit in our lives rather than to argue about our different modes of apprehending him. Directly we begin to chide each other for orthodoxy or unorthodoxy we cease to be the catholic body we are: for the logical end of such chiding is sanctions and the excluding of the weaker body by the stronger. Let us keep our different modes of apprehension and remember always that it is the same God we serve, revealing himself to each according to his faith, his openness and his need.

Earlier, I quoted from Yukio Irie, whose language is so simple and so fresh, coming to Christ as he does from a Buddhist background. A few sentences further he says, "One need not define our father cleverly so long as one believes in him and follows him with affection."[1] Returning to Gerald Hibbert and repeating him,

> Of one thing we can be certain—there are depths beneath depths, and heights above heights in the Personality of Jesus which make rash generalizations or superficial solutions absurd. We are standing before the

[1] *Sharing the Quaker Faith*, ed. E. B. Bronner, 1959, p. 123.

greatest character in history and we may well hesitate before trying to express him in a formula.

We shall therefore expect and welcome diversity in our belief about Christ, and find unity in Christian discipleship. "The way is one", wrote Isaac Penington; "Christ the truth of God; and he that is in the faith, and in the obedience to that light which shines from his spirit into the heart of every believer, hath a taste of the one heart and of the one way, and knoweth that no variety of practices, which is of God, can make a breach in the true unity."[1]

We shall never find unity in insistence on any formulation of belief, but it will be found in self-giving commitment in response to his compelling call, "Follow thou me."

[1] *Christian Faith and Practice*, 1960, para. 222.

# SWARTHMORE LECTURES
## PREVIOUS TO 1940

QUAKERISM: A RELIGION OF LIFE.
By RUFUS M. JONES, M.A., D.Litt. (Out of print.)

SPIRITUAL GUIDANCE IN THE EXPERIENCE OF THE SOCIETY OF FRIENDS. By WILLIAM C. BRAITHWAITE, B.A., LL.B.

THE COMMUNION OF LIFE.
By DR. JOAN M. FRY. Second Edition.

HUMAN PROGRESS AND THE INWARD LIGHT.
By THOMAS HODGKIN, D.C.L. (Out of print.)

THE NATURE AND PURPOSE OF A CHRISTIAN SOCIETY.
By T. R. GLOVER, M.A. Fourth Impression.

SOCIAL SERVICE: ITS PLACE IN THE SOCIETY OF FRIENDS.
By JOSHUA ROWNTREE. (Out of print.)

THE HISTORIC AND THE INWARD CHRIST.
By EDWARD GRUBB, M.A. (Out of print.)

THE QUEST FOR TRUTH.
By SILVANUS P. THOMPSON, F.R.S. Third Edition.

THE MISSIONARY SPIRIT AND THE PRESENT OPPORTUNITY.
By HENRY T. HODGKIN, M.A., M.B.

THE DAY OF OUR VISITATION. By WILLIAM LITTLEBOY.

THE NEW SOCIAL OUTLOOK. By LUCY FRYER MORLAND, B.A.

SILENT WORSHIP: THE WAY OF WONDER.
By L. VIOLET (HODGKIN) HOLDSWORTH. Third Impression.

QUAKERISM AND THE FUTURE OF THE CHURCH.
By HERBERT G. WOOD, M.A.

THE NATURE AND AUTHORITY OF CONSCIENCE.
By RUFUS M. JONES, M.A., D.Litt. (Out of print.)

THE LONG PILGRIMAGE: HUMAN PROGRESS IN THE LIGHT OF THE CHRISTIAN HOPE. By T. EDMUND HARVEY, M.A.

RELIGION AND PUBLIC LIFE. By CARL HEATH.

PERSONAL RELIGION AND THE SERVICE OF HUMANITY.
By HELEN M. STURGE.

THE INNER LIGHT AND MODERN THOUGHT.
By GERALD K. HIBBERT, M.A., B.D. Second Impression.

THE QUAKER MINISTRY. By JOHN W. GRAHAM, M.A.

THE THINGS THAT ARE BEFORE US.
By A. NEAVE BRAYSHAW, B.A., LL.B.

CHRIST AND THE WORLD'S UNREST. By H. T. SILCOCK, M.A.

THE LIGHT OF CHRIST. By JOHN S. HOYLAND, M.A.

SCIENCE AND THE UNSEEN WORLD.
By ARTHUR STANLEY EDDINGTON, F.R.S. Sixth Impression.

DEMOCRACY AND RELIGION: A STUDY IN QUAKERISM.
By DR. G. SCHULZE-GAEVERNITZ. Second Impression.

CREATIVE WORSHIP. By HOWARD H. BRINTON, Ph.D. Second Impression.

EDUCATION AND THE SPIRIT OF MAN. By FRANCIS E. POLLARD, M.A.

UNEMPLOYMENT AND PLENTY.
By SHIPLEY N. BRAYSHAW, M.I.Mech.E. Third Impression.

CHRIST, YESTERDAY AND TO-DAY.
By GEORGE B. JEFFERY, F.R.S. Second Impression.

OUR RESPONSE TO GOD. By WILLIAM E. WILSON, B.D. Second Impression.

TOWARDS A NEW MANNER OF LIVING.
By DR. HOWARD E. COLLIER. Second Impression.

RELIGION AND CULTURE. By CAROLINE C. GRAVESON, B.A.

DEMOCRATIC LEADERSHIP. By A. BARRAT BROWN, M.A.

THE TRUSTWORTHINESS OF RELIGIOUS EXPERIENCE.
By D. ELTON TRUEBLOOD, Ph.D. Second Impression.

# GEORGE ALLEN AND UNWIN LTD

# GEORGE ALLEN & UNWIN LTD
*London: 40 Museum Street, W.C.1*

*Auckland: 24 Wyndham Street*
*Bombay: 15 Graham Road, Ballard Estate, Bombay 1*
*Buenos Aires: Escritorio 454-459, Florida 165*
*Calcutta: 17 Chittaranjan Avenue, Calcutta 13*
*Cape Town: 109 Long Street*
*Hong Kong: F1/12 Mirador Mansions, Kowloon*
*Ibadan: PO Box 62*
*Karachi: Karachi Chambers, McLeod Road*
*Madras: Mohan Mansions, 38c Mount Road, Madras 6*
*Mexico: Villalongin 32-10, Piso, Mexico 5, DF*
*Nairobi: PO Box 4536*
*New Delhi: 13-14 Asaf Ali Road, New Delhi 1*
*São Paulo: Avenida 9 de Julho 1138-Ap. 51*
*Singapore: 36c Princep Street, Singapore 7*
*Sydney, N.S.W.: Bradbury House, 55 York Street*
*Tokyo: 3 Kanda-Ogawamachi, 3-Chome*
*Toronto: 91 Wellington Street West*